grill it

recipes **+** techniques **+** cooking tips

MURDOCH BOOKS

contents

the basics

Grilling is probably one of the oldest cooking techniques and is certainly one of the simplest. At its core, grilling involves cooking food by putting it in contact with direct heat — either above or below the food. Grilling can be used to cook a wide range of foods, from meats, poultry and seafood, to vegetarian dishes and even desserts. The golden-brown colour that grilled foods attain is due to the process of caramelization of starches and sugars that occurs during cooking, so not only does grilling make food look appetizing, it also enhances its taste and aroma. There are three distinct grilling methods: cooking under the heat (broiling); cooking over direct heat, using a barbecue, chargrill pan or griddle; and using a covered grill. You can use these various grilling techniques to cook a whole three-course meal, or just a portion of it. Whichever method you use, grilling is a sure-fire way to stoke the appetite.

under the grill

Cooking food under the grill (broiler) is the simplest method of grilling. The grill can be powered either by gas or electricity, and is generally a separate component of the oven situated beneath the stovetop, although some ovens have the heat coil built into the ceiling of the oven. Food is placed under the heat source, and is cooked from above by radiant heat. Commercial kitchens refer to grills as salamanders, which get much hotter than domestic grills and are not part of the oven.

When food is cooked under the grill of the oven, it is usually placed on the oven grill tray, which sits under the heat coil. The grill tray has slits in it and rests on or in a grill pan, which catches any fat released from the food during cooking. Baking trays are also handy when cooking under the grill. Grilling can be an ideal form of cooking for people watching their fat intake.

over the grill

In over-the-grill cooking, food is placed directly over the heat — most popularly on an outdoor barbecue, which can be fired by gas, electricity, wood, charcoal or briquettes. A grill plate or flat plate is positioned over the heat source, and the heat is controlled to give a constant temperature. A chargrill plate — a heavy, metal barbecue plate containing slotted grill bars — imparts an authentic, smoky, unmistakeable barbecue flavour to food, as the food is directly exposed to the heat and fire through the grill bars. A chargrill flavour can also be achieved by cooking food in a chargrill pan, or on a griddle — a moveable flat, heavy, metal plate that can be used on the stovetop or on a barbecue.

Portable grills used in the kitchen sit on the benchtop and are powered by electricity. They are efficient for cooking small quantities of food for two to four people, and dismantle easily for cleaning. They follow the same principle of grilling as the large outdoor barbecue, and generally have a temperature gauge on the side for easy heat regulation.

covered grill

Covered grills include kettle-type barbecues and larger barbecues with hoods. The heat source — such as fuel briquettes — is positioned on two opposite sides of the base grill to provide indirect heat. These barbecues can be used without the lid for direct grilling, but lowering the lid provides an oven-like environment that enables you to cook larger pieces of meat and also speeds up the cooking time. A covered grill can also be used to smoke food, adding exquisite flavour and tenderness.

A drip tray is used in kettle barbecues for cooking food over indirect heat. It is placed between the fuel briquettes to trap any juices dripping down off the food. It also helps prevent flare-ups and makes cleaning up easier.

tools to get you sizzling

Grilling is a simple form of cooking that doesn't require the use of too many implements and gadgets, but you'll find long-handled cooking tongs, a heavy-duty spatula and basting brushes indispensable, as well as scrapers and scrubbing brushes for cleaning up after the event. Oven mitts are essential for handling hot plates or dishes direct from the grill; barbecue mitts, which are longer than oven mitts, protect more of the arm from the intense heat of the barbecue. If you regularly use a covered grill to roast chicken or large joints of meat, it's probably a good idea to invest in a meat thermometer, which takes all the guesswork out of testing when the meat is cooked.

Fish lovers may find a fish grill useful — a fish-shaped cage or basket that holds the fish intact during grilling over direct or indirect heat and makes it easy to turn the fish during cooking. A wire grill basket is handy for holding smaller pieces of meat or vegetables together and lets you flip all the food over in one easy action. Some have long handles for use over open flames. Vegetable racks (which have prongs to hold vegetables in place) and warming racks can also be useful.

Metal, wooden and bamboo skewers are used to cook small (usually cubed) pieces of meat, fish and vegetables together and are an attractive way to present food. You'll need to soak wooden skewers in water for at least 30 minutes before use so the heat doesn't scorch them too quickly. To stop the ends burning, a simple but effective trick is to wrap aluminium foil around them. If you're using metal skewers, oil them before threading food onto them for easier removal later. If you regularly grill food on skewers, you might want to buy some skewer holders to keep the skewers raised up off the barbecue plate to ensure that the food doesn't burn.

If you run out of skewers, make your own: lemon grass stems, split lengths of sugarcane and long, well-washed sprigs of rosemary make beautiful skewers and have the added bonus of imparting a wonderful flavour to the food. (You'll need to soak sugarcane strips for about an hour before use.)

getting ready to grill

Food is best cooked when it reaches room temperature, so take it out of the refrigerator 20–30 minutes before you wish to cook it. However, don't leave food sitting at room temperature for too long or it will become a haven for bacteria, particularly in hot weather. Also, for even cooking, ensure large joints of meat are completely thawed before you start to cook, and cut food into similar-sized portions so it will all cook at the same rate — the bigger the pieces, the longer they'll take to cook.

Seasoning vegetables with a coarse salt (such as sea salt) prior to grilling will intensify their flavour and sweetness by drawing out moisture and concentrating their natural sugars. However, it is best to season meat just before or after it's cooked. If you season it too far ahead of time, the salt will draw out all the juices, leaving the meat disappointingly dry.

Par-boiling some foods that have a high fat content, such as sausages and ribs, can reduce the cooking time and minimize the risk of flare-ups from fat dripping into the fire or igniting on a grill tray.

Rubs, butters, marinades, bastes and crusts are simple ways to add flavour to food and to keep it moist (see pages 384–393 for some fabulous flavour boosters). When applying a rub to large cuts of meat, first cut shallow slashes into the thickest portions to enable all the flavours to penetrate. Red meats are best marinated for at least 1 hour to allow the flavours to soak in, but the flavours will become more intense if the meat is marinated for up to 8 hours or overnight. Chicken can be marinated for 1–2 hours or overnight. Fish and seafood are often marinated in mixtures containing lemon or lime juice. Where large quantities of lemon or lime juice are used, the seafood should not be marinated for longer than about 30 minutes, as the acid in the juice will start 'cooking' the flesh.

the heat is on

When putting food on or under the grill, take care not to overcrowd the grill — leave a little space between each item, or the food may stew in its own juices. During grilling, avoid piercing food with a knife or fork as it will lose precious juices and become dry and tough. Use long-handled tongs or a spatula to turn food.

When brushing hot food with oil, avoid using plastic-bristled brushes as the bristles will melt. To make your own basting brush, tie together a bunch of fresh herbs (such as rosemary and thyme), dip the tips in oil and run it over the food. It adds flavour and is bound to impress your guests!

If you're using a marinade and wish to use it as a baste during cooking, you'll need to first boil it and let it simmer for at least 5 minutes to stop any bacteria from the raw meat being transferred to the cooking meat. When cooking foods that have been steeped in sweetened marinades, use a medium heat so as not to burn the sugar.

Before carving grilled red meats, pork and poultry, let them rest. Cover them loosely with foil and leave in a warm place for 5–10 minutes. This helps the muscle fibres in the meat to relax, making the meat more tender and juicy.

basting brushes

Available in a variety of sizes, these handy brushes are
indispensable for brushing oil over food before cooking to
stop it sticking to your hotplate, and for basting food with
marinades and roasting juices during cooking.

scrubbing brushes

Stiff-wire brushes have durable metal bristles to dislodge food particles and grit from the barbecue hotplate, leaving the surface smooth and clean, ready for oiling.

scrapers

Metal scrapers take the hard work out of cleaning a barbecue hotplate once you've finished cooking. Many different types are available — some with flat blades, others with grooves for getting down the sides of barbecue slats.

tongs, spatulas, skewers

Tongs and spatulas are used for turning food during cooking, keeping fingers well away from flames and fierce heat. Metal skewers are terrific when you don't have time to soak wooden skewers — and they don't burn on the barbecue, either!

caring for your grill

Don't leave a grill dirty as the metal will **corrode**. After cooking, turn up the burners to **burn** off food, turn off the heat and scrub the plate clean.

To quickly clean a hot grill, you can **drizzle** it with lemon juice and **rub** it with lemon halves.

Leftover beer is **good too** — just pour it over and **scrape** off the dirty bits with a metal scraper.

As soon as the grill has cooled down a little, **wipe some oil** over the grill and flat plate to help protect the metal. **Remove** any ash or embers.

17

under the grill

under fire

Cooking under the grill (broiler) is the most basic form of grilling, and simply involves putting food directly under the heat coil or element of your oven. Most oven grills are a separate component located above the oven, beneath the stovetop, but some grills are incorporated into the top of the oven itself. Many marvellous dishes are given extra 'oomph' from being flashed under the grill: exposing the surface of the food to intense radiant heat sears the top, keeping the juicy goodness inside and concentrating all the flavours. Cooking under the grill is the perfect way to whip up something tasty with a minimal amount of effort. The ever-popular cheese on toast is probably the classic under-the-grill dish, but you might be surprised at just how many extraordinarily delicious dishes can be prepared this way, from enticing little starters and supremely tasty snacks to substantial main-course big-on-flavour hunger-busters and elegant desserts.

starting out

There aren't too many tricks you need to master to get the best results from cooking food under the grill. Mostly it's just a matter of getting to know your particular grill. As a general rule, always preheat the grill to the right temperature before you start to cook. It is also important to ensure that both the grill tray and grill pan are completely clean and free from bits of food which can burn under heat and taint the flavour of your food.

Bear in mind that oil and cooking fats are highly combustible, so to avoid any possibility of dangerous flare-ups, drain excess fat from your food before you start cooking to stop it catching fire under the hot grill. Also, keep a watchful eye on the grill when cooking food with a high fat content, such as sausages. Most types of sausages can be parboiled before grilling to reduce their fat content.

Make sure the top of the food isn't sitting too close to the top of the grill or the food will scorch under the intense heat. You should also check to see that the food is sitting in an even layer so that it cooks through consistently. Remember that many grills have 'hot spots', so you might find it necessary to move the food around so that the top browns evenly. But by the same token, make sure the food isn't too far away from the heat source as some foods may start to stew, rather than grill. If you find some portions of food are starting to brown too quickly, cover them lightly with foil while cooking the rest. This is a simple and effective way to stop them burning.

a time saver

To save on washing up, the grill tray can be covered with aluminium foil when grilling vegetables such as capsicums (peppers), which release a lot of liquid that tends to burn onto the grill tray. However, when grilling meats, poultry or seafood, it is best to leave the grill tray uncovered and allow any oil or fat to drip into the grill pan underneath — you can still save on washing up by lining the actual grill pan with aluminium foil. When you've finished grilling and the element and grill tray have cooled, simply bundle up the cold foil and discard it.

goat's cheese and pear toasts

makes 20

1 long **breadstick**, cut into 20 slices

100 g (3 1/2 oz) **quince paste**

2 **corella pears**, quartered and cored

150 g (5 1/2 oz) log **goat's cheese**

extra virgin olive oil, to serve

Heat the grill (broiler) to high. Spread the bread slices on the grill tray and toast under the hot grill for a few minutes on both sides, until lightly golden. Allow to cool, then spread with the quince paste.

Cut each pear quarter lengthways into 5 thin slices and arrange 2 pear slices on each slice of toast. Cut the goat's cheese log into 20 thin slices (don't worry if it crumbles a little), and arrange on top of the pear slices.

Cook the toasts under the hot grill for about 1 minute to warm and soften the cheese — it won't melt completely. Drizzle with extra virgin olive oil, season with cracked black pepper and serve hot.

tip These are terrific as a canapé, or you could make 18 instead of 20 toasts and serve three to a plate with some dressed baby frisée (curly endive) or rocket (arugula) as a simple starter for six. If corella pears are not available, just use any smallish pear.

honey and lime prawn kebabs with mango salsa

serves 4 as a starter

3 tablespoons **clear runny honey**

1 small **red chilli**, seeded and
  finely chopped

2 tablespoons **olive oil**

grated **zest** and **juice** of 2 **limes**

1 large **garlic clove**, crushed

2 cm (3/4 inch) piece fresh **ginger**,
  peeled and finely grated

1 tablespoon chopped **coriander**
  (cilantro) leaves

32 **tiger** or **king prawns (shrimp)**,
  peeled and deveined, tails intact

mango salsa

2 **tomatoes**

1 small **just-ripe mango**, diced

1/2 small **red onion**, diced

1 small **red chilli**, seeded and
  finely chopped

grated **zest** and **juice** of 1 **lime**

2 tablespoons chopped **coriander**
  (cilantro) leaves

In a small bowl, whisk together the honey, chilli, oil, lime zest and lime juice, garlic, ginger and coriander. Put the prawns in a non-metallic dish, add the marinade and toss well. Cover and refrigerate for several hours, turning the prawns occasionally.

Before you start cooking, soak eight bamboo skewers in cold water for 30 minutes. While the skewers are soaking, make the salsa. Score a cross in the base of each tomato and put them in a heatproof bowl. Cover with boiling water, leave for 30 seconds, then plunge in cold water and peel the skin away from the cross. Remove the seeds, dice the flesh, saving any juices, and put the tomato with all its juices in a bowl. Mix in the mango, onion, chilli, lime zest, lime juice and coriander.

Heat the grill (broiler) to high. Thread 4 prawns onto each skewer and grill for 4 minutes, or until pink and cooked through, turning halfway through cooking and basting regularly with the leftover marinade. Serve at once with the salsa.

tip When threading the prawns on the skewers, don't squash them too closely together as they may not cook through properly.

stuffed mushrooms with a pine nut salad

serves 4 as a starter

8 large **field mushrooms**

2 tablespoons **olive oil**

2 **vine-ripened tomatoes**, seeded
and chopped

2 tablespoons shredded **basil leaves**

2 tablespoons snipped **chives**

150 g (5¹/2 oz) **goat's cheese**, crumbled

3 thin slices **prosciutto**, cut into
short strips

pine nut salad

200 g (7 oz) **baby rocket (arugula)
leaves**

300 g (10¹/2 oz) jar **marinated
artichokes**, quartered (reserve
3 tablespoons of the marinade)

2 tablespoons **extra virgin olive oil**

1 **garlic clove**, crushed

2 tablespoons toasted **pine nuts**

Heat the grill (broiler) to very hot. Trim the stems of the mushrooms level with the caps. Brush the tops of the mushroom caps with half the oil, then place them gill-side-down on the grill tray. Cook for 2 minutes, then turn the mushrooms over, brush the gills with the remaining oil and cook for a further 2 minutes.

Remove the mushrooms from the heat and top with the tomato, basil and chives. Season with salt and pepper, then scatter with the crumbled goat's cheese and prosciutto. Grill for another 2 minutes, or until the prosciutto is crisp. Keep warm.

While the mushrooms are grilling, assemble the pine nut salad. Arrange the rocket and artichokes on four large plates. In a small bowl, whisk the reserved artichoke marinade with the oil and garlic until well combined. Season to taste, then drizzle the dressing over the salad and sprinkle with the pine nuts. Arrange 2 cooked mushrooms on each plate and serve hot.

thai chicken and mango skewers

makes 6

lime and sweet chilli marinade

4 tablespoons **lime juice**

4 tablespoons **fish sauce**

3 tablespoons **caster (superfine) sugar**

3 tablespoons **sweet chilli sauce**

1 1/2 tablespoons **peanut oil**

4 tablespoons chopped **coriander (cilantro) leaves**

1 tablespoon finely chopped **lemon grass**, white part only

750 g (1 lb 10 oz) **chicken thigh fillets**, trimmed and diced into
   3 cm (1 1/4 inch) cubes

2 very firm **mangoes**, peeled and cut into 3 cm (1 1/4 inch) cubes

6 **lime wedges**

Soak six bamboo skewers in cold water for 30 minutes. Meanwhile, put all the lime and sweet chilli marinade ingredients in a large, shallow non-metallic bowl and mix together well. Add the chicken, toss well to coat all over, then cover and marinate in the refrigerator for 20 minutes, turning once or twice.

When you're nearly ready to eat, heat the grill (broiler) to medium. Thread 4 chicken cubes and 3 mango cubes onto each bamboo skewer in an alternating fashion. Place the skewers slightly apart on a lightly greased grill tray and grill for about 8–10 minutes, or until the chicken is golden brown all over and cooked through, turning once during cooking and basting occasionally with the marinade. Serve the skewers hot with the lime wedges.

tip If you have time, the chicken can be marinated for up to 3 hours to enhance the flavour.

chunky parmesan toasts

makes 24

125 g (4¹/2 oz) **butter**, softened

65 g (2¹/2 oz/²/3 cup) finely grated **parmesan cheese**

1 tablespoon finely snipped **chives**

1 small whole loaf **white sandwich bread**, cut into 12 thick slices

Heat the grill (broiler) to high. Meanwhile, combine the butter, cheese and chives in a small bowl and mix well. Spread each slice of bread with the butter mixture and arrange the slices on the grill tray. Cook for about 1–2 minutes, or until the tops are lightly golden. Slice the toasts in half and serve immediately, while crispy and hot.

tip You can vary this recipe by adding garlic or even a little chilli to the butter. Alternatively, use finely chopped basil along with the chives for a really fresh herb flavour.

oysters rockefeller

makes 24

24 **oysters** on the half-shell

rock salt, for stacking

60 g (2¼ oz) **butter**

2 slices **bacon**, finely chopped

8 **English spinach leaves**, finely chopped

2 **spring onions (scallions)**, finely chopped

2 tablespoons finely chopped **flat-leaf (Italian) parsley**

4 tablespoons **dry breadcrumbs**

dash of **Tabasco sauce**

Arrange the oysters in their shells on a bed of rock salt in a baking tray — the salt will hold the oysters steady and stop the filling falling out later during grilling. Cover and refrigerate until needed.

Heat the grill (broiler) to high. Meanwhile, melt the butter in a frying pan, then add the bacon and cook over medium heat for about 2 minutes, or until browned. Add the spinach, spring onion, parsley, breadcrumbs and a dash of Tabasco and cook for about 1 minute, or until the spinach has wilted.

Spoon the mixture onto the oysters and grill for 2–3 minutes, or until the topping is golden. Serve immediately, while hot.

sage and bocconcini pots

makes 6

250 g (9 oz) **baby bocconcini (fresh mozzarella) cheese**, quartered

3 tablespoons **crème fraîche**

1 tablespoon finely chopped **sage leaves**

2 tablespoons finely grated **parmesan cheese**

6 thin slices **pancetta**

Heat the grill (broiler) to medium. Divide the bocconcini quarters among six lightly oiled 125 ml (4 fl oz/1/2 cup) ramekins.

In a small bowl, combine the crème fraîche, sage and parmesan, season with freshly ground black pepper and mix well. Spoon the mixture evenly into the ramekins, and top each with a slice of pancetta.

Put the ramekins on the grill tray and cook for about 1–2 minutes, or until the pancetta is lightly browned and the cheese has softened slightly. Serve hot.

garlic bread and olive skewers

makes 12

125 ml (4 fl oz/1/2 cup) **extra virgin olive oil**

2 **garlic cloves**, crushed

2 teaspoons finely chopped **rosemary leaves**

3 tablespoons finely grated **parmesan cheese**

425 g (15 oz) loaf **crusty Italian bread**, crust removed

100 g (31/2 oz) **pitted green olives**

100 g (31/2 oz) **pitted black olives**

Soak 12 bamboo skewers in cold water for 30 minutes. Heat the grill (broiler) to high.

Put the oil, garlic, rosemary and parmesan in a large bowl, season with sea salt and mix together well.

Chop the bread into bite-sized cubes and toss them through the garlic oil mixture. Thread the bread and olives alternately onto the skewers and grill for 2–3 minutes, turning occasionally, until the bread is deliciously golden. Serve hot.

otak-otak

makes 14

2 small **dried red chillies**

14 **banana leaf** portions, each

16 x 12 cm (6¹/4 x 4¹/2 inches)

450 g (1 lb) skinless **fish fillets** (such

as groper, hapuka, blue warehou,

halibut, haddock or snapper)

1 stem **lemon grass**, cut into thirds

1 small **onion**, peeled and halved

1 large **garlic clove**, peeled

generous pinch of **ground turmeric**

1 teaspoon **palm sugar** or

soft brown sugar

1 teaspoon **ground coriander**

1 teaspoon **shrimp paste**

1 tablespoon **candlenuts, peanuts**

or unsalted **macadamia nuts**

1 tablespoon chopped **mint**

1 tablespoon chopped **coriander**

(cilantro) leaves

3 tablespoons **coconut milk**

Put 14 toothpicks in a bowl, cover with cold water and leave to soak. Put the dried chillies in a small bowl, cover with boiling water and leave to soak.

If the banana leaves have been frozen they will be soft when thawed, but if they are fresh and tough, blanch them in boiling water for a minute to soften, then drain and refresh in cold water.

Roughly chop the fish and put in a food processor. Blend to a thick purée, then transfer to a mixing bowl. Drain the chillies and remove any stalks. Put the chillies in the processor with a generous pinch of salt and all the remaining ingredients except the banana leaves. Blend to a paste, then gently mix through the puréed fish.

Heat the grill (broiler) to medium, and drain the cocktail sticks. Put 2 tablespoons of the fish mixture in the middle of each banana leaf. Enclose the filling by folding the shorter sides into the middle so that they overlap. Tuck the two protruding ends underneath to make a small parcel. Secure the two ends with a cocktail stick.

Put the parcels on a baking tray, smooth-side-up, and grill for 5 minutes, or until the parcels are hot in the middle. Serve hot, or as a chilled snack.

tip Make sure your banana leaves are well folded and tucked in or they may unfold as they cook, but try not to fold them too tightly as the filling needs a little room to expand. If you can't obtain banana leaves, use foil instead.

mushroom melts

serves 6 as a starter

1 large **red capsicum (pepper)**

6 **field mushrooms** (about 7 cm/2³/4 inches in diameter)

60 g (2¹/4 oz/¹/4 cup) ready-made **pesto**

60 g (2¹/4 oz/¹/2 cup) grated **cheddar cheese**

6 slices **sourdough** or **woodfired bread**

2–3 tablespoons **extra virgin olive oil**

2–3 **garlic cloves**, peeled and cut in half

chives, to serve

Heat the grill (broiler) to high. Cut the capsicum into large flat pieces, discarding the seeds and membrane. Arrange skin-side-up on the grill tray and grill until the skin blackens and blisters. Leave to cool in a plastic bag, then peel away the skin and roughly chop the flesh. Turn the grill down to medium.

Arrange the mushrooms gill-side-up on the grill tray and spread with the pesto. Sprinkle with the capsicum and cheddar and season with freshly ground black pepper. Grill for 3–5 minutes, or until the cheese has melted and turned a light golden brown — you may need to grill the mushrooms in two batches. When you're done, remove the mushrooms from the heat and leave to cool slightly.

Put the bread slices on the grill tray and toast lightly on both sides. Lightly drizzle both sides of the bread with the oil, then gently rub all over with a cut garlic clove. Sit the mushrooms on the toasts and serve at once, topped with chives if desired.

salmon, ricotta and red onion frittata

serves 4–6

2 **red onions**, cut into 5 mm (1/4 inch) thick slices

2 tablespoons **olive oil**

150 g (5¹/2 oz) **baby English spinach leaves**

8 **eggs**

2 **spring onions (scallions)**, finely chopped

200 g (7 oz) sliced **smoked salmon**

100 g (3¹/2 oz) **ricotta cheese**

light sour cream, to serve

Heat the grill (broiler) to high. Spread the onion on a lightly greased oven tray, lightly brush with some of the oil and grill for 2–3 minutes, or until nicely browned. Gently flip the onions over, brush with a little more oil if needed and grill for another 2–3 minutes. Remove from the tray and set aside. Turn the grill down to medium.

While the onion is grilling, bring a saucepan of water to the boil. Add the spinach and blanch for 30 seconds, then drain and refresh in cold water. Squeeze out any liquid and roughly chop the leaves.

Beat the eggs in a bowl, season with salt and pepper, then stir in the spinach and grilled onion. Heat the remaining oil in a 21 cm (8¹/4 inch) non-stick frying pan, add the spring onion and sauté over medium heat for about 1 minute, or until soft. Stir the spring onion through the egg mixture, then pour the mixture back into the pan. Roll the smoked salmon slices into small rosettes and arrange them around the frittata. Spoon small dollops of ricotta in between the salmon rosettes.

Cook the frittata on the stovetop over medium heat for about 10 minutes, moving the pan around over the heat to ensure even cooking. When the frittata is cooked halfway through, put the pan under the grill and cook for 5–10 minutes, or until the top is golden brown and the frittata is cooked through. If the frittata starts to brown too quickly, cover it with a sheet of foil.

Slide or invert the frittata onto a plate, slice it into wedges, sprinkle with cracked black pepper and serve warm with a dollop of sour cream.

sausage and sweet potato wraps

serves 4

1 tablespoon **olive oil**

400 g (14 oz) **orange sweet potato**, peeled and thinly sliced

1 large **zucchini (courgette)**, cut lengthways into 4 pieces

4 **thick beef sausages**

4 pieces **lavash bread**

75 g (2 1/2 oz/1/3 cup) ready-made **hummus**

175 g (6 oz/1 cup) ready-made **tabouleh**

sweet chilli sauce, to serve

Heat the grill (broiler) and grill tray to medium. Pour the oil into a bowl and season with salt and pepper. Add the sweet potato and zucchini, gently toss the vegetables about to coat, then arrange them in a single layer on the preheated grill tray — you will probably need to work in two batches. Grill the vegetables for 5 minutes, then flip them over and cook for another 5 minutes, or until tender. Remove and set aside.

Arrange the sausages on the grill tray and grill for 10–12 minutes, turning once, until browned all over and cooked through. Set aside to cool for 5 minutes, then cut the sausages in half lengthways.

To assemble the wraps, spread each lavash bread with 1 tablespoon of hummus and 3 tablespoons of tabouleh. Top with the sweet potato, zucchini and the sausage halves, drizzle with sweet chilli sauce, then roll up and serve.

bagels with poached eggs and tomato hollandaise

serves 4

8 **asparagus spears**, trimmed and halved on the diagonal

1 tablespoon **vinegar**

8 **eggs**

4 **bagels**, split in half

200 g (7 oz) **shaved ham**

tomato hollandaise

2 tablespoons **cider vinegar**

2 tablespoons **white wine**

10 **peppercorns**

2 **parsley stalks**

2 **egg yolks**

200 g (7 oz) **butter**, melted

1 small ripe **tomato**, peeled and seeded, flesh finely chopped

1 tablespoon finely snipped **chives**

Blanch, steam or microwave the asparagus until tender. Drain, refresh in a bowl of iced water and set aside.

To make the tomato hollandaise, put the vinegar, wine, peppercorns and parsley stalks in a small saucepan and simmer for 2 minutes, or until reduced to 1 tablespoon. Discard the peppercorns and parsley stalks. Put the mixture in a heatproof bowl with the egg yolks and place over a saucepan of simmering water. Whisk until the mixture starts to thicken (take care not to overcook at this point or you will end up with scrambled eggs). Remove the pan from the heat and gradually add the melted butter a few drops at a time, then in a thin stream, whisking well until all the butter is incorporated (discard the white milky liquid at the base of the butter). Stir in the tomato and chives, season to taste and keep warm.

Heat the grill (broiler) to high. Meanwhile, half-fill a deep frying pan with water, add the vinegar and bring to a gentle simmer. Crack each egg, one at a time, into a small bowl before gently sliding them into the pan. Simmer until the egg whites turn opaque, then carefully remove the eggs with a spatula and keep warm.

Put the split bagels on an oven tray and toast both sides under the hot grill for about 4 minutes, or until lightly browned. Top each bagel with ham and briefly grill again to warm the ham. Top each bagel with a poached egg, arrange two drained asparagus strips over the top and add a dollop of tomato hollandaise. Grill for about 2 minutes, or until the hollandaise is golden and bubbling. Serve at once.

Refresh the asparagus
in a bowl of **iced water**
to stop the cooking process.

Add the melted butter to the
hollandaise **a few drops**
at a time, whisking constantly.

pork and lime skewers

serves 4

50 g (1 3/4 oz) shaved **palm sugar** or **soft brown sugar**

250 ml (9 fl oz/1 cup) **light coconut cream**

1 **bird's eye chilli**, seeded and finely chopped

grated **zest** of 1 large **lime**

3 tablespoons **lime juice**

1 **makrut (kaffir lime) leaf**, finely shredded (see tip)

750 g (1 lb 10 oz) **pork fillets**, cut into 2 cm (3/4 inch) cubes

4 **lime wedges**

Soak eight bamboo skewers in cold water for 30 minutes. Meanwhile, put the sugar, coconut cream and chilli in a saucepan and stir over low heat until the sugar has dissolved. Pour into a large non-metallic bowl, allow to cool a little, then add the lime zest, lime juice and makrut leaf. Add the pork, toss gently, then cover and marinate in the refrigerator for 20 minutes, turning occasionally.

Heat the grill (broiler) to medium. Thread the pork onto the skewers, reserving the marinade. Spread the skewers slightly apart on an oiled grill tray, then grill for 8–10 minutes or until cooked through, turning once.

While the pork is sizzling, put the reserved marinade in a small saucepan. Bring to the boil, then reduce the heat and simmer for 5 minutes. When the pork is done, spoon the sauce over the skewers and serve with the lime wedges. Delicious with rice.

tip When shredding a makrut (kaffir lime) leaf, first remove the large fibrous vein running down the middle of the leaf. An easy way to do this is to fold the leaf in half lengthways, then chop away the centre vein with a knife.

semolina with three cheeses

serves 6–8

500 ml (17 fl oz/2 cups) **chicken stock**

750 ml (26 fl oz/3 cups) **milk**

250 g (9 oz/2 cups) **fine semolina**

1 **egg yolk**

75 g (2 1/2 oz/3/4 cup) finely grated **parmesan cheese**

2 1/2 large handfuls **parsley**, finely chopped

50 g (1 3/4 oz) **mild gorgonzola cheese**, crumbled

60 g (2 1/4 oz/1/2 cup) coarsely grated **cheddar cheese**

4 tablespoons **thickened (whipping) cream**

Pour the stock and milk into a large saucepan. Stir together, bring to the boil, then remove from the heat. Add the semolina in a slow, steady stream, whisking constantly to prevent lumps forming. Put the pan back over medium heat and whisk for about 3 minutes, or until the mixture has boiled and is very thick (it will now be difficult to whisk). Turn off the heat. Working quickly and using a wooden spoon, beat in the egg yolk, parmesan and parsley and season to taste with salt and freshly ground pepper.

Spread the mixture into a lightly oiled, shallow, 2.5 litre (87 fl oz/10 cup) baking dish. Stand at room temperature for about an hour, or until firm.

Heat the grill (broiler) to medium. Turn the semolina out onto a board, but keep the baking dish handy. Using a wet knife, trim the edges of the semolina. Cut the semolina in half lengthways, then into eight long rectangles. Now cut each piece in half diagonally to form 16 triangles and place on a lightly oiled baking tray. Grill for 7 minutes on each side, or until nicely browned. Turn the grill up high.

Arrange the semolina triangles, in two slightly overlapping rows, back in the baking dish. Sprinkle evenly with the gorgonzola and cheddar and drizzle with the cream. Put the baking dish under the grill and cook for 5 minutes, or until the cheese is hot and bubbling. Serve warm, sprinkled with a good grind of cracked black pepper.

japanese chicken omelettes

serves 4

2 x 200 g (7 oz) **chicken breast fillets**, trimmed

8 **eggs**

1 tablespoon **soy sauce**

1 tablespoon **sesame seeds**

100 g (3½ oz) **snowpeas (mangetout)**, finely julienned

1 small **daikon**, finely julienned

1 small **carrot**, finely julienned

100 g (3½ oz/1 punnet) **snowpea (mangetout) sprouts**

soy and sesame dressing

1 tablespoon **soy sauce**

4 tablespoons **rice vinegar**

2 teaspoons **sesame oil**

Arrange the chicken breasts in a single layer in a large shallow saucepan. Add enough cold water to cover by about 3 cm (1¼ inches). Bring to a very slow simmer, then cook over low heat for 10 minutes. Turn the heat off and allow the chicken to cool in the cooking liquid.

Whisk the soy and sesame dressing ingredients together in a bowl and season to taste with salt and pepper. Finely shred the cooled chicken breasts and gently toss through the dressing until coated all over.

Heat the grill (broiler) to medium. Whisk the eggs and soy sauce together in a jug. Put a lightly oiled 26 cm (10½ inch) non-stick frying pan on the stovetop over medium heat. When the pan is hot, pour in a quarter of the egg mixture and swirl it around the base and sides, then quickly remove from the heat and sprinkle with 1 teaspoon of the sesame seeds. Put the pan under the grill for about 1 minute, or until the omelette is lightly browned. Slide the omelette onto a large plate and cover with foil to keep warm. Repeat with the remaining egg mixture and sesame seeds to make four omelettes.

Divide the chicken, snowpeas, daikon and carrot among the omelettes, then fold in the sides to enclose the filling. Serve at once on a bed of snowpea sprouts.

couscous with grilled fennel

serves 4

4 **baby fennel bulbs**, with fronds

olive oil, for brushing

2 **red onions**, each cut into 8 wedges

250 ml (9 fl oz/1 cup) **chicken** or **vegetable stock**

140 g (5 oz/3/4 cup) **couscous**

preserved lemon dressing

1 **preserved lemon quarter**

4 tablespoons **virgin olive oil**

1/2 teaspoon **Dijon mustard**

11/2 tablespoons **lemon juice**

For the best **flavour**, choose firm **fennel** with luscious, healthy green fronds.

Fluff up the couscous with a fork, **raking out** any lumps.

Bring a saucepan of water to the boil. Meanwhile, trim the fronds from the fennel bulbs. Chop up enough fronds to fill a tablespoon and reserve for the couscous. Remove the stalks from the fennel and cut a 5 mm (1/4 inch) thick slice off the base of each bulb. Cut the bulbs into quarters, then add them to the pan of boiling water. Cook, covered, for about 3 minutes, or until tender. Drain well.

Heat the grill (broiler) to medium. Lightly brush the grill tray with oil and spread the fennel and onion wedges over the top, taking care not to crowd them. Brush the vegetables with a little olive oil and grill for 10 minutes, or until tender and lightly coloured, turning the vegetables during cooking.

While the vegetables are grilling, make the preserved lemon dressing. Scoop out and discard the flesh from the preserved lemon. Wash the rind thoroughly, then pat dry and finely chop. In a small bowl, whisk the oil, mustard and lemon juice together until combined. Add the preserved lemon and season to taste.

To prepare the couscous, bring the stock to the boil in a saucepan. Stir in the couscous and reserved chopped fennel leaves and take the pan off the heat. Cover and leave for 4–5 minutes, then fluff up the couscous with a fork, raking out any lumps. Transfer the couscous to a serving dish and arrange the grilled fennel and onion wedges over the top. Drizzle the dressing over the top and serve.

grilled salmon with fennel and orange salad

serves 4

fennel and orange salad

1 **fennel bulb**, with fronds

2 **oranges**, peeled and segmented

12 **pitted black olives**

1 tablespoon snipped **chives**

3 tablespoons **virgin olive oil**

2 tablespoons **lemon juice**

1 teaspoon **Dijon mustard**

1/2 teaspoon **caster (superfine) sugar**

500 g (1 lb 2 oz) piece **salmon fillet**

1 tablespoon **virgin olive oil**

200 g (7 oz) **baby English spinach leaves**

To prepare the salad, trim the fronds from the fennel bulb and finely chop up enough fronds to fill a tablespoon. Remove the stalks from the fennel and cut a 5 mm (1/4 inch) thick slice off the base of the bulb. Cut the bulb in half, then finely slice and toss in a large bowl with the chopped fronds, orange segments, olives and chives. In a separate bowl, whisk the oil with the lemon juice, mustard and sugar. Season to taste, pour over the fennel mixture and toss gently to coat.

Heat the grill (broiler) to medium. Remove the bones and skin from the salmon and cut the flesh into 1 cm (1/2 inch) thick slices. Put the salmon in a shallow dish, add the oil, and season with salt and pepper. Toss gently to coat, then place on a lightly greased grill tray. Grill for 1–2 minutes, or until just cooked through.

Divide the spinach leaves among four large serving plates, top with the fennel and orange salad and arrange the salmon over the spinach. Serve warm.

tip Fennel bulbs are easily sliced using the slicing disc of a food processor.

chilli capsicum gnocchi with goat's cheese

serves 4–6

chilli capsicum gnocchi

1 large **red capsicum (pepper)**

500 g (1 lb 2 oz) **orange sweet potato,**
peeled and chopped

500 g (1 lb 2 oz) old **potatoes,**
peeled and chopped

1 tablespoon **sambal oelek**

1 tablespoon grated **orange zest**

340 g (11 3/4 oz/2 3/4 cups) **plain**
(all-purpose) flour

2 **eggs**, lightly beaten

500 g (1 lb 2 oz/2 cups) ready-made
tomato-based pasta sauce, warmed

100 g (3 1/2 oz) **goat's cheese,**
crumbled

2 tablespoons finely chopped
basil leaves

Heat the grill (broiler) to high. Cut the capsicum into large flat pieces and remove the seeds and membranes. Grill, skin-side-up, until the skin blackens and blisters, then turn off the grill. Put the capsicum in a plastic bag and leave to cool. Peel off the skin, then put the flesh in a food processor and blend to a smooth purée.

Meanwhile, cook the sweet potato and potato in a large saucepan of boiling water for 10–15 minutes, or until very soft. Drain, transfer to a large bowl and mash until smooth.

To make the gnocchi, add the capsicum purée to the mashed potato mixture with the sambal oelek, orange zest, flour and eggs and mix to form a soft dough. Using floured hands, roll heaped teaspoons of the dough into oval gnocchi shapes. Gently press the top of each gnocchi with the prongs of a lightly floured fork.

Bring a large saucepan of salted water to a rapid boil. Add the gnocchi in batches and cook until they float to the surface, then cook for a further 3 minutes. Remove with a slotted spoon and divide between warmed, shallow ovenproof serving bowls. Reheat the grill to high. Spoon the warm pasta sauce over the top of the gnocchi, sprinkle with the crumbled goat's cheese and grill for 1–2 minutes, or until the cheese is just lightly browned. Sprinkle with the basil and serve.

sausage skewers with lemon olive salsa

serves 4

4 **thin pork sausages**

4 **thin Italian sausages**

1/2 **lemon**, cut into 8 wedges

lemon olive salsa

2 tablespoons **extra virgin olive oil**

1 **garlic clove**, crushed

zest of 1 **lemon**

21/2 teaspoons **thyme leaves**

90 g (31/4 oz/1/2 cup) **Ligurian olives**

1 small **red capsicum (pepper)**, finely chopped

thyme sprigs, to serve

Soak eight bamboo skewers in cold water for 30 minutes. Meanwhile, put the sausages in a large saucepan, cover with water and bring to the boil. Reduce the heat and simmer for 5 minutes, then drain and set aside to cool.

Put the salsa ingredients in a small bowl, mix together well, then season with salt and freshly ground pepper and set aside.

Heat the grill (broiler) to medium. Slice each sausage on the diagonal into four evenly sized diamond shapes. Thread 2 pork sausage pieces onto a skewer, then add 1 lemon wedge, piercing it through the rind first rather than the flesh, then finish off with 2 Italian sausage pieces. Repeat with the remaining skewers.

Put the skewers on the grill tray and cook for 3 minutes on each side, or until golden. Serve hot with the salsa, garnished with thyme sprigs.

salad pizzas

makes 6

pizza bases

2 teaspoons **dried yeast**

1/2 teaspoon **caster (superfine) sugar**

215 g (71/2 oz/13/4 cups) **plain (all-purpose) flour**

1/4 teaspoon **salt**

1/2 teaspoon **dried oregano**

1 tablespoon **olive oil**

salad topping

60 g (21/4 oz/1/2 cup) ready-made **sun-dried tomato pesto**

125 g (41/2 oz/1 cup) grated **swiss cheese**

1 tablespoon **balsamic vinegar**

2 tablespoons **olive oil**

1 **garlic clove**, crushed

100 g (31/2 oz) **mixed lettuce leaves**

1 **Lebanese (short) cucumber**, sliced lengthways into long thin ribbons

95 g (31/2 oz/1/2 cup) small **black olives**

30 g (1 oz/1/4 cup) roughly chopped **roasted hazelnuts**

Put the yeast and sugar in a small bowl. Quickly stir in 170 ml (5½ fl oz/⅔ cup) of tepid water, then cover and leave in a warm place for 10–15 minutes, or until the mixture is foamy. (If the mixture doesn't foam, the yeast is dead and you will need to start again.)

Sift the flour, salt and oregano into a large bowl, make a well in the centre and add the yeast mixture and oil. Knead on a lightly floured surface to form a soft dough. Place in an oiled bowl, cover and leave in a warm place for about 30 minutes, or until doubled in size.

Heat the grill (broiler) to medium. To make the pizza bases, punch the dough down and divide it into six portions. Roll or press each portion on a lightly floured surface into a thin 15 cm (6 inch) round. Place on a lightly oiled oven tray and brush with a little more oil. Prick all over with a fork and grill for 1–2 minutes, or until puffed and lightly browned, then turn and repeat on the other side. Keep them warm while you finish cooking the remaining pizza bases in the same way.

To prepare the topping, lightly spread the pizza bases with the pesto, sprinkle with swiss cheese and grill for 1–2 minutes to melt the cheese. Put the vinegar, oil and garlic in a small screw-top jar and shake well to combine. Mix the lettuce, cucumber and olives in a bowl, add the dressing and toss lightly. Arrange the salad on top of the pizza bases, sprinkle with the hazelnuts and serve at once.

Turn the dough onto a lightly floured work surface and **knead** until **soft.**

When the dough has doubled in size, **punch it down** with your knuckles.

grilled cheesy club sandwich

serves 4

4 slices **bacon**, halved

125 g (4½ oz/½ cup) **mayonnaise**

1 **garlic clove**, crushed

1 tablespoon **lemon juice**

12 thin, large slices **country-style** or **sourdough bread**

2 **tomatoes**, sliced

10 thin slices **swiss** or **jarlsberg cheese**

1 ripe **avocado**, coarsely mashed

Heat the grill (broiler) to high. Put the bacon on the grill tray and grill for about 2 minutes on each side, or until lightly browned but not crisp.

Meanwhile, mix together the mayonnaise, garlic and lemon juice and season well with freshly ground black pepper.

Put 8 bread slices under the grill and toast on one side only for about 1 minute, or until golden. Sit 4 of the slices on a work surface, toasted-side-down. Spread the tops with half the garlic mayonnaise, then add the tomato slices, then a slice of cheese. Put an untoasted slice of bread on top of each, spread with the remaining garlic mayonnaise and sit a bacon slice on top. Spread with the avocado, then top with the remaining slices of grilled bread, placing them toasted-side-up. Press each sandwich down firmly to compact the filling. Arrange 1½ slices of cheese on top of each toasted sandwich, allowing the cheese to fall over the sides a little.

Return the sandwiches to the grill and cook for 1 minute, or until the cheese bubbles and browns. Cool slightly, then cut in half diagonally. Serve warm.

creamy ratatouille with farfalle

serves 6

350 g (12 oz) **baby eggplants (aubergines)**

6 **garlic cloves**, crushed

3 tablespoons **olive oil**

1 large **red capsicum (pepper)**

1 large **green capsicum (pepper)**

1 **onion**, diced

400 g (14 oz) tin **diced tomatoes**

2 **zucchini (courgettes)**, finely diced

1 tablespoon **thyme leaves**, chopped

3 tablespoons **parsley**, chopped

3 tablespoons **red wine**

1 tablespoon **soft brown sugar**

2 teaspoons **tomato paste (purée)**

2 1/2 handfuls **basil leaves**, plus extra whole leaves, to serve

500 g (1 lb 2 oz) **farfalle** pasta

100 ml (3 1/2 fl oz) **cream (whipping)**

Heat the grill (broiler) to high. Cut the ends off the eggplants and slice the flesh lengthways into 2 cm (3/4 inch) strips. Spread on a baking tray lined with foil. In a bowl, mix 1/2 teaspoon of the crushed garlic with 1 tablespoon of the oil and brush over the eggplant. Grill for about 3–5 minutes, or until golden brown, then remove.

Cut the capsicums into large flat pieces and remove the seeds and membranes. Cook, skin-side-up, under the hot grill until the skin blackens and blisters. Leave to cool in a plastic bag, then peel away the skin and cut the flesh into strips.

Heat the remaining oil in a large frying pan. Add the onion and remaining garlic and gently sauté for 3 minutes. Stir through the grilled eggplant, capsicum, tomato, zucchini, thyme, parsley, wine, sugar, tomato paste and basil leaves. Season well, then simmer, uncovered, for 30 minutes, stirring occasionally.

While the ratatouille is simmering, cook the pasta in a large saucepan of rapidly boiling salted water until *al dente*. Drain well and keep warm.

Take the ratatouille off the heat, add the cream and stir through gently. Divide the pasta among six serving bowls and spoon the ratatouille over the top. Garnish with the extra basil leaves and serve.

shellfish with foaming citrus butter

serves 4

1 kg (2 lb 4 oz) **live moreton bay bugs (flat head lobsters)** (see tip)
sourdough or **country-style bread**, to serve

foaming citrus butter

50 g (1¾ oz) **butter**
1 large **garlic clove**, crushed
1 tablesoon finely grated **orange zest**
1 tablespoon **blood orange juice** or **regular orange juice**
1 tablespoon **lemon juice**
1 tablespoon finely snipped **chives**

Freeze the bugs for 1–2 hours before cooking. Nearer to cooking time, heat the grill (broiler) to its highest setting.

Plunge the semi-frozen bugs into a large saucepan of boiling water for 2 minutes, then drain. Using a sharp knife or cleaver, cut each bug in half from head to tail. Put the bugs on a large baking tray, cut-side-up. Grill for 5–6 minutes, or until the flesh turns white and opaque, turning halfway through cooking.

Meanwhile, make the foaming citrus butter. Melt the butter in a small saucepan and when sizzling, add the garlic. Cook over medium heat for 1 minute, stirring. Stir in the orange zest, orange juice and lemon juice and bring to the boil. Add the chives and season with salt and pepper.

Divide the bugs among four serving plates, and serve the foaming citrus butter in small individual bowls for everyone to dip their shellfish and bread in. Finger bowls and napkins are also a good idea!

tip Instead of moreton bay bugs (flat head lobsters) you could use live slipper lobsters or crayfish for this recipe. You may need to boil them for a slightly longer time to cook them, and you'll need to remove the heads before slicing them down the middle. Depending on their size, they may also need a little longer under the grill (broiler).

chicken thighs with persian spice mix

serves 4

8 **chicken thigh fillets**, trimmed

grated **zest** and **juice** of 2 **limes**

170 ml (5¹/2 fl oz/²/3 cup) **olive oil**

1 tablespoon **coarse black pepper**

2¹/2 handfuls **basil leaves**, shredded

lime wedges, to serve

persian spice mix

¹/2 teaspoon **cumin seeds**

¹/2 teaspoon **ground turmeric**

1 teaspoon grated **lemon zest** (see tip)

2 **cardamom pods**

4 **black peppercorns**

Place the chicken thighs between two sheets of plastic wrap and gently flatten with a rolling pin. Mix the lime zest, lime juice, oil, pepper and basil in a non-metallic bowl and season with salt. Add the chicken, toss well to coat all over, then cover and marinate in the refrigerator for 2 hours.

Put all the Persian spice mix ingredients in a spice grinder with a good pinch of salt and blend to a fine powder. (You could also use a mortar and pestle if you're feeling energetic.)

Heat the grill (broiler) to medium. Drain the chicken from the marinade and sprinkle with the spice mix. Spread the chicken on the grill tray and grill for 8 minutes on each side, or until cooked through. Serve hot with lime wedges.

tip For a highly authentic Persian flavour, instead of the lemon zest use ¹/2 teaspoon of green mango powder (also called amchoor), if you can find it. Ready-made Persian spice mix is also sold in some speciality food stores.

grilled asparagus and zucchini lasagne

serves 4

500 g (1 lb 2 oz) **asparagus spears**, trimmed

500 g (1 lb 2 oz) **zucchini (courgettes)**, sliced lengthways into
  5 mm (1/4 inch) thick ribbons

2 tablespoons **olive oil**

6 large (20 x 15 cm/8 x 6 inch) **fresh lasagne sheets**

150 g (51/2 oz/1 cup) grated **mozzarella cheese**

white sauce

500 ml (17 fl oz/2 cups) **milk**

50 g (13/4 oz) **butter**

50 g (13/4 oz) **plain (all-purpose) flour**

125 ml (4 fl oz/1/2 cup) **cream (whipping)**

pinch of **grated nutmeg**

Heat the grill (broiler) to medium. Put the asparagus and zucchini in a large bowl, add the oil and gently toss to coat. Spread on a large baking tray and grill in batches for 2–3 minutes, or until lightly chargrilled and cooked, turning during cooking. Remove and leave to cool a little, then cut the asparagus into shorter lengths.

Bring a large saucepan of water to the boil. Add some salt and bring to the boil again. Add the lasagne sheets and stir gently with a wooden spoon. Boil for about 5–7 minutes, or until the water boils again and the pasta is al dente (the cooking time will vary according to the thickness of your lasagne sheets). Drain into a large colander, then carefully lay the sheets on a clean tea towel to dry.

Preheat the oven to 180°C (350°F/Gas 4). Meanwhile, make the white sauce. Gently heat the milk in a small saucepan and set aside. In another saucepan, melt the butter and stir in the flour. Cook over medium heat, stirring with a wooden spoon, for about 3 minutes. Gradually add the milk and stir for 5 minutes, or until the sauce becomes smooth and boils and thickens. Remove from the heat and stir through the cream and nutmeg. Season with salt and white pepper to taste.

Lay 2 pasta sheets in a lightly oiled 20 x 30 cm (8 x 12 inch) baking dish and trim off any excess. Pour a little white sauce over the top and spread it about evenly. Arrange a layer of grilled vegetables on top, then spread with some more of the white sauce. Repeat to form another two layers, then scatter the grated mozzarella over the top. Bake for 45 minutes, or until the cheese is golden brown.

Grill the zucchini and asparagus in batches until **lightly chargrilled** and cooked.

Stir the white sauce with a **wooden spoon** until it becomes smooth and thick.

grilled pork with quince and fig salad

serves 4

600 g (1 lb 5 oz) **pork fillet**

3 tablespoons **quince jam** (see tip)

8 fresh **figs**, halved

1 teaspoon **fennel seeds**

50 g (13/4 oz) **baby rocket (arugula) leaves**

2 tablespoons **olive oil**

1 tablespoon **balsamic vinegar**

Heat the grill (broiler) to medium. Rub the pork fillet all over with the quince jam and place on a lightly oiled, foil-covered baking tray. Put the tray under the grill and cook the pork for 10 minutes, ensuring it is not too close to the heat source or the jam may burn. Turn the pork over and cook for 10 minutes more, or until just cooked through. Remove the pork, cover loosely with foil and leave to rest.

While the pork is resting, sprinkle the figs evenly with the fennel seeds and grill for 3–5 minutes, or until softened. Remove from the heat and allow to cool.

Slice the pork diagonally and gently toss in a large bowl with the figs, rocket, oil and vinegar. Season to taste with salt and pepper and serve.

tip Quince jam is sold in tins in Middle Eastern grocery stores, and in small tubs in some delicatessens and speciality shops.

spiced quail with grilled plums

serves 4

8 cleaned **quail**, at room temperature

4 **red plums**, halved

25 g (1 oz) **butter**, melted

1 1/2 tablespoons **caster (superfine) sugar**

1/2 teaspoon **five-spice powder**

spicy marinade

3 tablespoons **soy sauce**

2 tablespoons **kecap manis**

2 tablespoons **Chinese rice wine**

2 tablespoons **peanut oil**

2 teaspoons **five-spice powder**

3 teaspoons finely grated fresh **ginger**

1 **garlic clove**, crushed

Using kitchen scissors, cut each quail down both sides of the backbone. Turn the quails over, skin-side-up, and gently flatten the centre of the birds with the palm of your hand. Using paper towels, clean out the insides. Rinse well and pat dry with paper towels.

Put the spicy marinade ingredients in a small bowl and mix together well. Pour into a large shallow dish, add the quail and brush well all over with the marinade. Cover and marinate in the refrigerator for 30 minutes, turning once.

Heat the grill (broiler) to high. Put the quail, breast-side-down, on a large lightly oiled grill tray, shaking off any excess marinade. Grill for 4 minutes, then turn over, baste with the marinade and grill for a further 4 minutes, or until cooked through. Transfer to a warm plate and cover loosely with foil.

Put the plums in a shallow tray and brush with the melted butter. Combine the sugar and five-spice powder and sprinkle over the plums. Grill for 3–5 minutes, or until the topping begins to caramelize. Serve the quail with the plums and any juice from the plums. Terrific with couscous or a salad of baby Asian greens.

lamb cutlets with a walnut and blue cheese crust

serves 4

175 g (6 oz) **creamy blue-vein cheese**

45 g (1 1/2 oz/1/3 cup) **walnuts**, chopped

1 1/2 tablespoons chopped **mint**

1–2 **garlic cloves**, crushed

12 **lamb cutlets**, trimmed

1 tablespoon **olive oil**

Put the cheese, walnuts, mint and garlic in a bowl and mash with a fork until well combined. Season with freshly ground black pepper.

Heat the grill (broiler) to high and line the base of the grill tray with foil. Lightly brush the cutlets with the oil and season with black pepper. Arrange them on the grill tray and cook for 4–8 minutes, or until browned.

Turn the cutlets over and roughly spread the cheese mixture over the top. Grill for another 2–4 minutes, or until the crust is browned and bubbling and the lamb is cooked to your liking. Serve with steamed green vegetables and baby potatoes.

fish tikka

serves 4

marinade

250 g (9 oz/1 cup) **thick plain yoghurt**

2 **spring onions (scallions)**, finely chopped

1 tablespoon grated fresh **ginger**

2 **garlic cloves**, crushed

2 tablespoons **lemon juice**

1 teaspoon **ground coriander**

1 tablespoon **garam masala**

1 teaspoon **paprika**

1 teaspoon **chilli powder**

2 tablespoons **tomato paste (purée)**

1 teaspoon **salt**

500 g (1 lb 2 oz) skinless **firm white fish fillets** (such as flake, sea bream, snapper, grouper or orange roughy)

2 **onions**, each cut into 8 chunks

2 small **green** or **red capsicums (peppers)**, each cut into 8 chunks

lemon wedges, to serve

yoghurt dressing

50 g (1¾ oz/about ⅓ cup) peeled, diced **cucumber**

1 tablespoon chopped **coriander (cilantro) leaves**

250 g (9 oz/1 cup) **thick plain yoghurt**

Mix all the marinade ingredients together in a shallow non-metallic dish long enough and deep enough to hold eight long metal skewers.

Cut the fish into 24 bite-sized chunks. On each skewer, thread 3 fish pieces, 2 onion pieces and 2 capsicum pieces, alternating them as you go. Turn the skewers about in the marinade so that all the fish and vegetables are well coated. Cover and marinate in the refrigerator for at least 1 hour, or overnight if convenient.

Mix the yoghurt dressing ingredients together in a small bowl and set aside.

Heat the grill (broiler) to its highest setting. When the grill is very hot, lift the skewers out of the marinade and grill for 5–6 minutes, or until the fish is firm and slightly charred. Serve with the yoghurt dressing and lemon wedges.

tip The grill needs to be very hot when cooking this dish to impart an authentic smoky, slightly charred tandoor-like flavour.

swiss-style chicken

serves 4

4 x 200 g (7 oz) **chicken breast fillets**

1 tablespoon **virgin olive oil**

40 g (11/2 oz) **butter**

1 **garlic clove**, crushed

200 g (7 oz) **button mushrooms**, sliced

1 tablespoon chopped **tarragon**

125 ml (4 fl oz/1/2 cup) **cream (whipping)**

1 tablespoon **brandy**

4 large slices **gruyère** or **swiss cheese**

Heat the grill (broiler) to high. Place the chicken breasts between two sheets of plastic wrap and pound with a mallet or rolling pin until 1 cm (1/2 inch) thick. Sit the chicken breasts slightly apart on a lightly oiled grill tray and brush them with the oil. Grill for about 5 minutes, or until cooked through, turning once during cooking. Transfer to a lightly oiled shallow ovenproof dish.

While the chicken is grilling, melt the butter in a frying pan. Add the garlic and mushrooms and cook over medium heat for 3 minutes, or until the mushrooms have softened. Add the tarragon, cream and brandy and stir over high heat for about 2 minutes, or until the sauce has reduced and thickened.

Spoon the hot sauce over the chicken breasts and top with a slice of cheese. Put the dish under the hot grill and cook for about 4 minutes, or until the cheese has melted. Serve hot.

vegetarian eggplant rolls

serves 4

tomato sauce

2 tablespoons **olive oil**

1 small **onion**, finely diced

1 **celery stalk**, finely diced

1/2 small **leek**, finely diced

2 **garlic cloves**, crushed

4 tablespoons **red wine**

400 g (14 oz) tin **diced tomato**

1 tablespoon **tomato paste (purée)**

1/2 teaspoon finely chopped **thyme leaves**

1/2 teaspoon finely chopped **oregano leaves**

1 teaspoon **soft brown sugar**

2 large **eggplants (aubergines)**

3 tablespoons **olive oil**

250 g (9 oz/1 cup) **ricotta cheese**

21/2 handfuls **basil leaves**, finely shredded

75 g (21/2 oz/1/2 cup) grated **mozzarella cheese**

Cut each eggplant into six **even slices**, discarding the end pieces.

Spread the chargrilled eggplant with ricotta and gently **roll up** from one end.

94

First, make the tomato sauce. Heat the oil in a saucepan, add the onion, celery and leek and cook, stirring, over medium heat for 5 minutes, or until they start to soften. Add the garlic and cook for another 1–2 minutes, or until the garlic starts to turn golden. Pour in the wine and cook for 4 minutes, or until it has almost evaporated. Stir in the tomato, tomato paste and herbs, then simmer over low heat, stirring frequently, for 15–20 minutes, or until the sauce has thickened. Stir in the sugar and add some salt and pepper to taste. Cover and keep warm until needed.

While the sauce is simmering, heat a chargrill pan to medium. Cut each eggplant lengthways into six evenly sized slices about 1 cm (1/2 inch) thick, discarding the end pieces or reserving them for another recipe. Lightly brush each slice with the oil. Working in batches, chargrill the eggplant slices for 1–2 minutes, then rotate them at right angles and cook for another 1–2 minutes to get a crisscross chargrill pattern underneath. Flip the slices over and repeat on the other side. Repeat with the remaining eggplant.

Heat the grill (broiler) to its highest setting. Put the ricotta in a bowl with two-thirds of the basil and mix until smooth. Season with salt and pepper. Spread the ricotta mixture evenly over each eggplant slice, then roll the slices up from one end and place seam-side-down in a shallow 18 x 22 cm (7 x 81/2 inch) ovenproof dish. Spoon the warm tomato sauce over the top and sprinkle with the grated mozzarella.

Put the dish under the hot grill and cook the rolls for 7 minutes, or until the cheese is golden and bubbling. Serve on a bed of freshly cooked egg fettucine, scattered with the remaining basil.

warm chinese pork with radish salad

serves 4

2 tablespoons **hoisin sauce**

2 tablespoons **soy sauce**

2 teaspoons **Chinkiang vinegar**
   (see tip)

2 tablespoons **honey**

1/2 teaspoon **five-spice powder**

4 large **pork loin chops**

radish salad

3 tablespoons **olive oil**

1 tablespoon **red wine vinegar**

1 teaspoon **Dijon mustard**

1 **garlic clove**, crushed

1/2 teaspoon **sugar**

1 **butter lettuce**, leaves torn

6 small **red radishes**, thinly sliced

4 **spring onions (scallions)**, thinly sliced

Put the hoisin sauce, soy sauce, vinegar, honey and five-spice powder in a large shallow dish. Mix together well, add the chops and turn to coat all over. Cover and refrigerate for several hours, or overnight, turning occasionally.

Heat the grill (broiler) to high. Place the chops on the grill tray and cook for about 5 minutes on each side, or until the marinade starts to caramelize. Remove the tray from the grill, cover loosely with foil, then leave the chops to rest for 5 minutes.

While the chops are resting, make the radish salad. Whisk the oil, vinegar, mustard, garlic and sugar in a bowl and season to taste. Put the lettuce, radish and spring onion in a large bowl, add the dressing and toss well. Serve with the warm chops.

tip Chinkiang vinegar is a mild Chinese black rice vinegar with a subtle smoky flavour. Look for it in Asian grocery stores.

lamb loin chops with artichoke and olive stuffing

serves 4

75 g (2¹/2 oz/1 cup) **coarse fresh breadcrumbs**, made from an Italian bread
   such as ciabatta

12 **pitted black olives**, roughly chopped

8 **marinated artichoke quarters**, roughly chopped (reserve 1 tablespoon
   of the marinade)

2 tablespoons chopped **flat-leaf (Italian) parsley**

¹/2 teaspoon finely grated **lemon zest**

8 **lamb loin chops**, with tails

Heat the grill (broiler) to high. To make the stuffing, put the breadcrumbs, olives, artichoke and reserved artichoke marinade in a bowl with the parsley and lemon zest. Mix lightly to combine.

Unroll the tails from the lamb chops and fill them with the stuffing. Roll the tails up to enclose the stuffing, then secure with a toothpick. Season with salt and pepper, place on the grill tray and grill for about 5–7 minutes on each side, or until cooked to your liking — the cooking time will vary according to thickness of your chops. Serve warm. Delicious with a salad of rocket (arugula) and avocado, dressed with olive oil and balsamic vinegar.

split sausages with caramelized onions and a gorgonzola topping

serves 4

caramelized onions

1 tablespoon **olive oil**

1 tablespoon **butter**

3 large **red onions**, thinly sliced

1 teaspoon **thyme leaves**, chopped

1 tablespoon **balsamic vinegar**

8 **thick beef sausages**

150 g (51/2 oz) **gorgonzola cheese**, crumbled

8 **thyme sprigs**

First, caramelize the onions. Heat the oil and butter in a saucepan, add the onion and stir over medium heat until the onion is well coated. Cook for 3–5 minutes, or until the onion starts to soften. Add the thyme, put the lid on and turn the heat to low. Cook for 40 minutes, stirring from time to time, until the onion becomes a deep, rich, golden brown. Add the vinegar and cook for another minute.

While the onion is caramelizing, heat the grill (broiler) to its highest setting. Put the sausages on a baking tray and grill for 5–10 minutes, turning them from time to time to ensure they brown all over.

Remove the sausages from the heat and split them down the middle, being careful not to cut all the way through. Fill the sausages with the caramelized onion, sprinkle the crumbled gorgonzola over the top, then grill for 1 more minute, or until the cheese has melted. Served warm, garnished with thyme sprigs. Excellent with a green leaf salad and baked jacket potatoes dolloped with some sour cream mixed with seeded mustard.

butterflied spatchcock with soft polenta

serves 4

4 x 500 g (1 lb 2 oz) **spatchcocks (poussin)**

4 tablespoons **olive oil**

1 tablespoon **balsamic vinegar**

2 tablespoons chopped **rosemary leaves**

1 tablespoon chopped **lemon thyme leaves**

1 large **lemon**, thinly sliced

rosemary sprigs, to serve

thyme sprigs, to serve

polenta

1 litre (35 fl oz/4 cups) **chicken stock**

150 g (5½ oz/1 cup) **instant polenta**

25 g (1 oz) **butter**

50 g (1¾ oz/½ cup) finely grated **parmesan cheese**

Cut each spatchcock down each side of the backbone using a large knife or kitchen shears. Discard the backbones, then remove and discard the necks. Turn the spatchcocks over and press down on the breastbone to flatten them out. Remove and discard any excess fat, skin and innards, then rinse well and pat dry with paper towels.

Put the oil, vinegar, rosemary, lemon thyme and lemon slices in a large bowl with some freshly ground black pepper. Mix well, add the spatchcocks and turn them about, ensuring the birds are thoroughly coated. Cover with plastic wrap and refrigerate for several hours or overnight.

Heat the grill (broiler) to medium. Put the spatchcocks, breast-side-down, on a large, oiled baking tray and season with sea salt. Grill for 15 minutes, then turn the birds over and grill for a further 15 minutes, or until well browned on both sides and cooked through. Remove from the heat, cover loosely with foil and leave to rest while preparing the polenta.

To make the polenta, bring the stock to the boil in a large saucepan. Add the polenta in a thin, steady stream, whisking constantly. Continue whisking over medium heat for about 5 minutes, or until the grains are tender. Remove from the heat, stir through the butter and parmesan and season to taste.

Spoon the polenta onto the side of four large serving plates. Sit the spatchcocks on the plates, scatter some rosemary and thyme sprigs over the top and serve.

tip This recipe is equally delicious with chicken breasts or even quail. Adjust the cooking time to suit the type of poultry used.

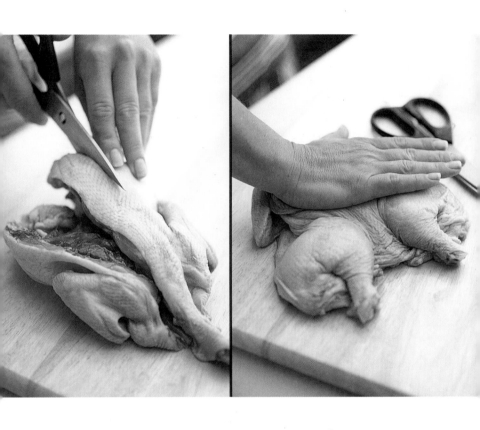

Carefully **cut** the **spatchcock** down each side of the backbone.

Press down on the breastbone with the **palm** of your hand.

lamb satay

makes 16

125 ml (4 fl oz/1/2 cup) **soy sauce**

4 tablespoons **Chinese rice wine**

2 **garlic cloves**, crushed

1 teaspoon grated fresh **ginger**

1 teaspoon **sesame oil**

600 g (1 lb 5 oz) **lamb backstraps**
   or **loin fillets**, cut into 3 cm
   (11/4 inch) chunks

4 **spring onions (scallions)**

satay sauce

2 teaspoons **peanut oil**

4 **red Asian shallots**, finely chopped

2 **garlic cloves**, crushed

2 teaspoons fresh **ginger**, grated

2 small **red chillies**, seeded and
   finely chopped

1/2 teaspoon **ground turmeric**

400 ml (14 fl oz) tin **coconut milk**

125 g (41/2 oz/1/2 cup) **crunchy
   peanut butter**

2 tablespoons grated **palm sugar**

2 tablespoons **lime juice**

11/2 tablespoons **fish sauce**

2 teaspoons **soy sauce**

1 **makrut (kaffir lime) leaf**

1 tablespoon chopped **coriander**
   (cilantro) leaves

Combine the soy sauce, rice wine, garlic, ginger and oil in a large bowl. Add the lamb and mix well to coat all over. Cover and refrigerate for 4 hours. Nearer to cooking time, soak 16 bamboo skewers in cold water for 30 minutes to prevent scorching.

To make the satay sauce, heat the oil in a saucepan, add the shallot, garlic, ginger and chilli and fry over medium heat for 5 minutes, stirring occasionally, until the shallots are soft and starting to turn golden. Add the turmeric and fry until fragrant. Add the coconut milk, peanut butter, sugar, lime juice, fish sauce, soy sauce and the whole makrut leaf. Bring to the boil, then reduce the heat and gently simmer for 7–10 minutes, stirring frequently, until the sauce is thick. Just before serving, remove the makrut and stir through the coriander.

While the sauce is simmering, heat the grill (broiler) to high. Cut the spring onions into 16 pieces about 3 cm (11/4 inches) long. Thread 1 spring onion strip and 2 meat chunks onto each skewer. Put the skewers on a lightly oiled grill tray and cook for 5 minutes, turning frequently. (If the ends of the skewers start burning, cover them with foil.) Serve at once with the satay sauce.

tuna with baked eggplant

serves 4

marinade
pinch of **saffron threads**
3 tablespoons **olive oil**
2 tablespoons **lemon juice**
1 tablespoon **pomegranate molasses**,
    optional (see tips)
1 small **onion**, grated
1 large **garlic clove**, crushed
1 tablespoon **dried oregano**
1 teaspoon **cumin seeds**
pinch of **kirmizi biber** (see tips),
    or **crushed dried chilli**

1 teaspoon **nigella seeds** (see tips), or
    1/2 teaspoon **cracked black pepper**
1 teaspoon **coriander seeds**, crushed

4 x 200 g (7 oz) **tuna fillets** (see tips)
1 small **eggplant (aubergine)**, chopped
80 g (2³/4 oz/1/2 cup) **toasted pine nuts**
100 g (3¹/2 oz) **lamb's lettuce (corn salad)**
2 tablespoons roughly torn **mint leaves**
3 tablespoons **olive oil**
1 tablespoon **red wine vinegar**
16 small **pitted black olives**

To make the marinade, soak the saffron in 1 tablespoon of hot water in a small bowl and leave to infuse for 10 minutes. Add a generous pinch of salt, then all the remaining marinade ingredients. Mix well. Put the tuna in a single layer in a shallow non-metallic dish and pour the marinade all over, ensuring the fish is thoroughly coated. Cover and refrigerate for 2 hours.

Heat the grill (broiler) to high. Lift the tuna fillets out of the marinade, reserving the marinade, and sit them on a large baking tray with the eggplant chunks. Brush the eggplant and fish all over with the marinade. Grill for 5–8 minutes, or until the fish is cooked, turning the eggplant occasionally.

Meanwhile toss the pine nuts, lettuce and mint in a bowl. Mix the oil with the vinegar, season to taste and toss through the salad. Divide the salad among four serving plates. Scatter with the olives and eggplant chunks and sit the tuna on top. Drizzle some of the cooking juices over the tuna and serve.

tips Pomegranate molasses is a syrup with a sweet and sour taste. Kirmizi biber is a chilli pepper spice, and nigella seeds are small black seeds with an aromatic flavour. They are often sold in Middle Eastern grocery stores. This recipe is also delicious with perch, sea bass and swordfish.

spicy chicken schnitzels

serves 4

4 x 200 g (7 oz) **chicken breast fillets**
1 tablespoon **ground coriander**
1 tablespoon **ground cumin**
1/2 teaspoon **chilli powder**, or to taste
2 **garlic cloves**, crushed
2 tablespoons **lemon juice**
2 tablespoons **olive oil**
250 g (9 oz/1 cup) **thick plain yoghurt**
1/2 teaspoon **harissa paste**, or to taste
1/2 teaspoon **caster (superfine) sugar**
2 tablespoons finely chopped **mint leaves**, plus extra sprigs, to serve

Place the chicken breasts between two sheets of plastic wrap and flatten them with a mallet or rolling pin until 11/2 cm (5/8 inch) thick.

In a small bowl, mix the ground coriander, cumin, chilli powder, garlic, lemon juice and oil together to form a paste. Thoroughly rub the paste all over the chicken fillets, then cover and leave to stand for 10 minutes.

Heat the grill (broiler) to high. Put the chicken on a lightly oiled grill tray and grill for 6–8 minutes, or until cooked through, turning once.

Meanwhile, blend 1 tablespoon of the yoghurt in a bowl with the harissa and sugar. Stir in the remaining yoghurt and mint, season to taste and serve with the warm chicken, garnished with extra mint sprigs. This dish is also delicious served cold.

classic mixed grill

serves 4

4 slices **bacon**, rind removed

4 **thin pork sausages**

30 g (1 oz) **butter**, softened

1 tablespoon snipped **chives**

1 tablespoon chopped **parsley**

4 large **flat mushrooms**, stems trimmed

4 **lamb cutlets**, trimmed

1 tablespoon chopped **rosemary leaves**

1 tablespoon **olive oil**, plus extra, for brushing

1/2 teaspoon **freshly ground black pepper**

2 large **tomatoes**, halved

8 thick slices **wholemeal (wholewheat) bread**

Heat the grill (broiler) and grill tray to medium. Wrap a piece of bacon around each sausage and secure with a toothpick. In a small bowl, combine the butter, chives and parsley. Sit the mushrooms on their caps and spoon the herb butter evenly all over the gills. Put the lamb, rosemary, oil and pepper in a bowl and mix together well. (If you have time, you could marinate the lamb for a while prior to grilling.)

Lightly brush the tomato halves with olive oil, sprinkle with salt and freshly ground pepper and place cut-side-up on the preheated grill tray with the sausages and lamb cutlets. Cook for 5–6 minutes, then turn the lamb and sausages. Add the mushrooms, gill-side-up, and cook for another 4 minutes. Remove the grill tray from the grill and cover loosely with foil to keep warm.

Spread the bread slices on a baking tray and toast under the grill for 2–3 minutes on each side, or until nicely browned. Divide the sausages, mushrooms, tomato and lamb cutlets among four serving plates and serve with the hot toast.

quail with a herb butter stuffing and rocket salad

serves 4

4 large cleaned **quail**, at room
temperature

100 g (3¹/2 oz) **unsalted butter**,
softened

2 tablespoons snipped **chives**

2 tablespoons finely chopped
lemon thyme leaves

1 **garlic clove**, crushed

olive oil, for brushing

4 **lime wedges**

rocket salad

2 tablespoons **olive oil**

1 tablespoon **balsamic vinegar**

¹/4 teaspoon **soft brown sugar**

¹/2 teaspoon **seeded mustard**

80 g (2³/4 oz) **baby rocket (arugula)**
leaves

50 g (1³/4 oz/¹/3 cup) **sun-dried**
tomatoes, thinly sliced

2 tablespoons chopped **roasted**
hazelnuts

Using kitchen scissors, cut each quail down both sides of the backbone. Turn the quails over, skin-side-up, and gently flatten the centre of the birds with the palm of your hand. Using paper towels, clean out the insides. Rinse well and pat dry with paper towels.

In a bowl, mix together the butter, chives, lemon thyme and garlic. Roughly divide the herb butter into four portions.

Heat the grill (broiler) to medium and line the grill tray with foil. Take a quail and gently loosen the skin over each breast with your finger. Slide a portion of the herb butter between the skin and breast, then repeat with the remaining birds. Put the quail on the grill tray, lightly brush with olive oil and season with salt and coarse black pepper. Grill for 5 minutes, then turn the birds over and grill for another 3 minutes, or until golden brown.

While the quail are cooking, make the rocket salad. Put the oil, vinegar, sugar and mustard in a small screw-top jar and shake until well combined. Put the rocket, tomato and hazelnuts in a bowl, add the dressing and toss well. Serve the warm quail with the lime wedges and salad.

gratin of crepes with pumpkin, goat's cheese and crisp sage leaves

serves 4

crepe batter

310 ml (10³/4 fl oz/1¹/4 cups) **milk**

50 g (1³/4 oz) **butter**

155 g (5¹/2 oz/1¹/4 cups) **plain (all-purpose) flour**

3 **eggs**

melted butter, for pan-frying

filling

400 g (14 oz) **butternut pumpkin (squash)**, peeled

2 tablespoons **olive oil**

125 ml (4 fl oz/¹/2 cup) **vegetable oil**

30 g (1 oz/1 bunch) **sage**, leaves plucked

250 g (9 oz) **soft goat's cheese**

topping

300 ml (10¹/2 fl oz) **cream (whipping)**

150 g (5¹/2 oz) **fontina cheese**, grated

Swirl the batter around the pan and cook for 30 seconds, or until **bubbles** appear.

Put the filling in one quarter of the crepe, then **fold up** carefully into a neat triangle.

To make the crepe batter, gently heat the milk and butter in a small saucepan until the butter has melted, but do not allow the milk to boil. Put the flour and a good pinch of salt in a large bowl and make a well in the centre. Add the eggs and slowly whisk in the warm milk mixture. Whisk until completely smooth — the mixture will be quite thin. Cover and leave to stand for 10–15 minutes.

Put a non-stick frying pan over medium heat. When hot, drizzle a little melted butter over the base. Add 60 ml (2 fl oz/1/4 cup) of the crepe batter and swirl to cover the base. Cook for 30 seconds, or until the crepe is set and bubbles start to appear. Using a spatula, carefully turn the crepe over and cook for another 30 seconds. Remove to a plate and continue until you have 12 perfect crepes. (It may take a bit of practice to get the crepes right, so if the first few don't turn out well don't worry, there's plenty of batter for 12 good crepes. Any leftover crepes can be used for another recipe.)

Heat a chargrill pan to medium. Cut the pumpkin into 24 slices, each about 1 cm (1/2 inch) thick. Put them in a large bowl with the olive oil and toss with ground pepper to coat. Chargrill the pumpkin in batches for 1–2 minutes, or until cooked through, turning once. Set aside to cool.

Put the vegetable oil in a small frying pan. Heat until the oil starts to haze — be careful not to let it burn. Quickly fry the sage leaves in batches until crisp, then remove and drain on crumpled paper towels.

Heat the oven grill (broiler) to its highest setting. Put 2 pumpkin slices, some goat's cheese and a few sage leaves in one quarter of each crepe, saving some sage leaves for the garnish. Fold the crepes up into neat triangles and divide among four ovenproof oval gratin dishes or shallow pasta dishes.

To make the topping, heat the cream in a small saucepan, then stir in the grated cheese. Pour the mixture evenly over the crepes. Sit the dishes on a large baking tray, put the tray under the grill and cook for 3–5 minutes, or until the cheese is bubbling and hot. Scatter with the reserved crispy sage leaves and serve.

tip The crepes can be made a day ahead. Cover them with plastic wrap and refrigerate until needed.

chargrilled tandoori lamb with cucumber salad and yoghurt dressing

serves 4

375 g (13 oz/1¹/2 cups) **thick plain yoghurt**

125 g (4¹/2 oz/¹/2 cup) ready-made **tandoori paste**

2 teaspoons **ground cumin**

2 **garlic cloves**, crushed

1 tablespoon **lemon juice**

12 **lamb cutlets**

yoghurt dressing

250 g (9 oz/1 cup) **thick plain yoghurt**

2 **garlic cloves**, crushed

1 tablespoon **olive oil**

1 tablespoon **lemon juice**

2 tablespoons finely chopped **mint**

cucumber salad

3 **Lebanese (short) cucumbers**, seeded and peeled into long, thin ribbons

300 g (10¹/2 oz/about ¹/2 bunch) **watercress**, picked over

3 tablespoons **extra virgin olive oil**

1¹/2 tablespoons **lemon juice**

In a large non-metallic bowl, mix together the yoghurt, tandoori paste, cumin, garlic and lemon juice with some salt and pepper. Add the lamb cutlets and toss well to coat. Cover and marinate for 2 hours, or overnight if possible.

Combine all the yoghurt dressing ingredients in a bowl and add salt and pepper to taste. Cover and refrigerate until needed.

Heat the grill (broiler) to high. Put the cutlets on the grill tray and cook for about 2–3 minutes on each side, or until done to your liking, basting with the marinade during cooking.

While the lamb is grilling, make the cucumber salad. Toss the cucumber and watercress in a large bowl. Put the oil and lemon juice in a small screw-top jar and shake until well combined, then season to taste. Drizzle the dressing over the salad, toss well and divide among four serving plates. Sit the cutlets on top and drizzle with the yoghurt dressing. Serve immediately.

chevapcici

serves 8

250 g (9 oz) **minced (ground) beef**
250 g (9 oz) **minced (ground) pork**
250 g (9 oz) **minced (ground) veal**
1/2 **onion**, grated
1 **clove garlic**, crushed
2 tablespoons finely chopped **dill**
1 tablespoon finely chopped **parsley**
11/2 teaspoons **ground coriander**
1/2 teaspoon **ground cumin**
1 teaspoon **paprika**

1 teaspoon **salt**
1/2 teaspoon **freshly ground black pepper**
1 teaspoon **baking powder**
3 tablespoons **beef stock**
25 g (1 oz/1/3 cup) **fresh breadcrumbs**
1 **egg**, lightly whisked

Put all the ingredients in a large bowl and thoroughly mix together with your hands.

Wet your hands in cold water to stop them sticking and divide the mixture into 16 equal portions. Roll the portions into sausage shapes about 12 cm (41/2 inches) long. Put them on a plate, then cover and refrigerate for 1 hour.

Heat the grill (broiler) to high. Sit the sausages on the grill tray and cook for about 6–8 minutes, turning often, until cooked through and evenly browned all over. Serve immediately, with tomato jam or your favourite relish or chutney.

grilled pork with spinach and blue cheese salad

serves 4

1 tablespoon **oil**

1–2 tablespoons **lime juice**

1 tablespoon grated fresh **ginger**

2 **spring onions (scallions)**, finely chopped

1 small **red onion**, finely chopped

400 g (14 oz) **pork fillet**, trimmed

spinach and blue cheese salad

150 g (5 1/2 oz) **baby English spinach leaves**

200 g (7 oz) good-quality **blue-vein cheese**, crumbled

70 g (2 1/2 oz/1/2 cup) **roasted hazelnuts**, chopped

extra virgin olive oil, for drizzling

Combine the oil, lime juice, ginger, spring onion and red onion in a shallow non-metallic dish. Season the mixture with salt and pepper and add the pork, turning to coat both sides. Cover and refrigerate for 15 minutes.

Heat the oven grill (broiler) to medium and line the grill tray with foil. Place the tray on the second shelf of the oven and grill the pork for 10 minutes. Turn the pork and grill for another 10 minutes for medium to well done. Remove from the oven, cover with foil and rest for 10 minutes.

While the pork is resting, assemble the salad. Arrange the spinach on a serving plate, then sprinkle with some of the cheese and nuts and drizzle with olive oil. Thinly slice the warm pork and serve on top of the salad. Sprinkle with the remaining cheese and nuts and serve.

carrot and almond salad

serves 4 as a side dish

4 large **carrots**

2 tablespoons **peanut oil**

1 teaspoon **caster (superfine) sugar**

1/2 teaspoon **brown mustard seeds**

1/4 teaspoon **curry powder**

2 tablespoons **lemon juice**

25 g (1 oz/1/4 cup) **toasted flaked almonds**

1 large handful **coriander (cilantro) leaves**

3 tablespoons **thick plain yoghurt**

Heat the grill (broiler) to medium. Slice the carrots thinly, on the diagonal. Put 1 tablespoon of the oil in a bowl, mix in the sugar, then add the carrot and toss to coat. Spread the carrot on a baking tray and grill for 10–15 minutes, turning occasionally, until lightly browned and tender. Remove from the heat and leave to cool, then place in a bowl.

While the carrots are grilling, heat the remaining oil in a small frying pan. Add the mustard seeds and curry powder and cook over low heat for 1 minute, or until fragrant. Allow to cool a little, then whisk in the lemon juice and season to taste.

Drizzle the spice mixture over the carrots, add the almonds and coriander and toss gently until well combined. Serve at room temperature, with a dollop of yoghurt.

tomato, eggplant and olive caponata

serves 4 as a side dish

3 firm **tomatoes**

5 **bulb spring onions (scallions)**, trimmed but not peeled

3 **slender eggplants (aubergines)**, cut lengthways into 5 mm (1/4 inch) thick slices

2 **red capsicums (peppers)**, quartered

50 g (13/4 oz/1/3 cup) **pitted kalamata olives**

1 tablespoon **toasted pine nuts**

3 tablespoons torn **mint leaves**

3 tablespoons **olive oil**

3 teaspoons **white wine vinegar**

1 teaspoon **caster (superfine) sugar**

1 **garlic clove**, crushed

Heat the grill (broiler) to high and line the grill tray with foil. Sit the whole tomatoes and onions on the rack of the grill tray and cook for about 10 minutes, turning often, until the tomato skins are charred in patches all over and start to split.

Remove the tomatoes from the heat and put the eggplant and capsicum on the rack, skin-side-up. Grill for about 8 minutes, or until well browned, turning the eggplant halfway through cooking. Remove all the vegetables from the grill and put the capsicum in a plastic bag to sweat.

Peel the tomatoes, cut them into 2 cm (3/4 inch) chunks and place in a colander to drain. Cut the eggplant into thick strips and put them in a bowl. When the capsicum is cool enough to handle, peel off the skin, then cut the flesh into strips. Halve the onions from top to bottom, then give them a light squeeze so that the centre pops out. Add the capsicum and onion to the eggplant along with the olives, pine nuts and mint and gently stir together.

Put the oil, vinegar, sugar and garlic in a small screw-top jar and shake well to combine. Season liberally with salt and black pepper and drizzle over the grilled vegetables. Add the drained tomato and toss lightly. Serve at room temperature.

grilled capsicum, pecan and herb salsa

serves 4 as a side dish

2 **red capsicums (peppers)**

2 **yellow capsicums (peppers)**

1 small **red chilli**, seeded and finely chopped

50 g (1³/4 oz/¹/2 cup) **pecan nuts**, halved lengthways

2 **spring onions (scallions)**, finely chopped

juice of 1 **lime**

2 tablespoons **virgin olive oil**

1 handful **mint leaves**

2 handfuls **coriander (cilantro) leaves**

thick plain yoghurt, optional, to serve

Heat the grill (broiler) to high. Cut the capsicums into large flat pieces and remove the seeds and membranes. Cook, skin-side-up, under the hot grill until the skin blackens and blisters. Leave to cool in a plastic bag, then peel away the skin and cut the capsicum into 2 cm (3/4 inch) squares.

Gently toss the capsicum in a serving bowl with all the remaining ingredients. Serve the salsa at room temperature, with a dollop of yoghurt if desired, seasoned with salt and freshly ground pepper.

grilled mixed mushrooms

serves 4 as a side dish

2 **field mushrooms**

150 g (5¹/2 oz/1¹/2 punnets) fresh **shiitake mushrooms**

100 g (3¹/2 oz/1 punnet) **enoki mushrooms**

150 g (5¹/2 oz/1 punnet) **oyster mushrooms**

150 g (5¹/2 oz/1 punnet) **shimeji mushrooms**

50 g (1³/4 oz) **butter**, melted

2 tablespoons **Japanese soy sauce**

1 tablespoon **mirin**

1 tablespoon chopped **flat-leaf (Italian) parsley**

Heat the grill (broiler) to medium. While the grill is heating, prepare the mushrooms. Discard the stems from the field mushrooms and cut the caps into quarters. Discard the stems from the shiitake mushrooms and cut the shiitake in half. Trim the hard ends off the enoki and pull apart the mushroom tops. Gently tear apart the oyster mushrooms. Remove the rough ends from the shimeji stems and gently pull apart the caps. Put all the mushrooms in a large bowl.

Combine the butter, soy sauce and mirin in a small bowl, pour over the mushrooms and toss to combine. Place the mushrooms in a shallow ovenproof dish, put the dish under the grill and cook the mushrooms for 5 minutes. Remove from the heat and gently toss the mushrooms with a pair of tongs, then grill for another 5 minutes. Serve hot, scattered with the parsley.

cauliflower and peas with a polonaise topping

serves 4 as a side dish

1 small **cauliflower**, cut into small florets

150 g (5 1/2 oz/1 cup) **fresh** or **frozen peas** (see tip)

polonaise topping

3 **hard-boiled eggs**

40 g (1 1/2 oz/1/2 cup) **fresh white breadcrumbs**

1 1/2 tablespoons **baby capers**, rinsed and drained

3 tablespoons finely chopped **flat-leaf (Italian) parsley**

1 **garlic clove**, finely chopped

75 g (2 1/2 oz) **unsalted butter**, melted

Heat the grill (broiler) to high. Add the cauliflower and peas to a large saucepan of lightly salted boiling water and simmer for about 5 minutes, or until tender. Drain the vegetables and arrange in a lightly oiled 26 x 18 cm (10 1/2 x 7 inch) gratin dish.

While the vegetables are cooking, make the polonaise topping. Mash the eggs in a bowl using a fork, then add the breadcrumbs, capers, parsley, garlic and melted butter. Mix well and season to taste with salt and freshly ground pepper. Sprinkle the topping all over the vegetables and grill for about 5–7 minutes, or until the breadcrumbs are golden and crunchy. Serve hot.

tip If you prefer to use fresh peas in this recipe, you will need to pod about 300 g (10 1/2 oz) fresh peas to get the right amount.

grilled pancetta, haloumi and cherry tomato salad

serves 4 as a side dish

100 g (3 1/2 oz) **pancetta**, thinly sliced

2 tablespoons **olive oil**

1 tablespoon **lemon juice**

1 **garlic clove**, crushed

1/2 teaspoon chopped **thyme leaves**

200 g (7 oz) **haloumi cheese**, cut into 1 cm (1/2 inch) thick slices

250 g (9 oz/1 punnet) **cherry tomatoes**

1 **baby cos (romaine) lettuce**, leaves torn

Heat the grill (boiler) to high. Spread the pancetta slices on the grill tray and cook for about 5 minutes, or until crisp but not too brown.

Put the oil, lemon juice, garlic and thyme in a small screw-top jar and shake well to combine. Season well with freshly ground black pepper and pour into a shallow dish. Add the haloumi and tomatoes and toss to coat.

Spread the haloumi and cherry tomatoes on the grill tray, reserving the dressing. Grill for about 8 minutes, or until the tomatoes split and are lightly browned, turning often. Remove the tomatoes and continue grilling the haloumi for another 3 minutes, or until browned on both sides.

Put the lettuce leaves in a serving bowl. Break the pancetta into smaller pieces and add to the lettuce along with the haloumi. Leave the tomatoes unpeeled, but discard any skins which have almost left the flesh. Add the tomatoes to the bowl with the reserved dressing and gently toss to coat. Season with salt and pepper if needed, then arrange the salad on four serving plates. Serve warm.

grilled eggplant with miso and parmesan

serves 4 as a side dish

6 **slender eggplants (aubergines)**

2 teaspoons **light olive oil**

1 1/2 tablespoons **white miso paste**

1 tablespoon **mirin**

1 **egg yolk**

2 tablespoons finely grated **parmesan cheese**

2 tablespoons snipped **chives**

Heat the grill (broiler) to high. Slice the eggplants in half lengthways and prick the skins several times with a fork. Brush the eggplant with the oil, place skin-side-up on the grill tray and grill for 10 minutes, turning once.

Remove the eggplant from the grill and arrange in a shallow ovenproof serving dish. Turn the grill down to medium.

Put the miso paste, mirin and egg yolk in a small bowl and whisk well to combine. Pour the mixture evenly over the surface of the eggplant and put the dish under the grill. Cook for 2 minutes, then sprinkle with the parmesan and grill for 1 minute more, or until the cheese starts to turn golden. Sprinkle with the chives and serve.

grilled green tomatoes with walnut crumble

serves 4–6 as a side dish

4 **green tomatoes** (see tip)

75 g (2¹/2 oz/1 cup) **coarse fresh breadcrumbs**, made from an Italian bread such as ciabatta

1 **garlic clove**, crushed

2 tablespoons roughly chopped **walnuts**

40 g (1¹/2 oz) **butter**, melted

2 tablespoons roughly chopped **flat-leaf (Italian) parsley**

1 tablespoon roughly chopped **oregano**

2 tablespoons grated **parmesan cheese**

Heat the grill (broiler) to medium. Cut each tomato into six wedges, remove the core and sit the wedges in a shallow, lightly oiled 17 x 26 cm (6¹/2 x 10¹/2 inch) ovenproof dish. Put the dish under the grill and cook the tomato for 5 minutes, or until heated through, turning the wedges over once during cooking.

Combine all the remaining ingredients in a bowl and add salt and pepper to taste. Sprinkle the mixture over the tomatoes and grill for another 5–6 minutes, or until the topping is golden brown and the tomatoes are hot.

tip The green tomatoes used in this recipe are simply unripe regular tomatoes. They can be difficult to find, so you may need to ask your greengrocer to order some in for you.

feta-filled zucchini

serves 6 as a side dish

6 **zucchini (courgettes)**

250 g (9 oz) **feta cheese**, crumbled

2 tablespoons snipped **chives**

1 **garlic clove**, crushed

2 1/2 tablespoons **olive oil**

6 **lemon wedges**

Put the whole zucchini in a saucepan of salted, boiling water and cook for about 6 minutes, or until just tender. Drain and leave to cool slightly.

Heat the grill (broiler) to high. Put the feta, chives and garlic in a small bowl with 1 tablespoon of the oil and freshly cracked black pepper to taste. Mix well.

When the zucchini are cool enough to handle, slice a strip about 5 mm (1/4 inch) deep from along the length of each zucchini and discard. Use a teaspoon to scoop out most of the seeds, and sit the zucchini cut-side-up on a lightly oiled baking tray.

Spoon equal amounts of the feta mixture into the cavity of each zucchini. Lightly brush each zucchini with a little of the oil and grill for about 10 minutes, or until lightly browned. Drizzle with the remaining oil, sprinkle with freshly cracked black pepper and serve with the lemon wedges.

tip This recipe can be prepared a day or two ahead. You can reheat the zucchini and serve them warm, but they are also delicious simply served cold on an antipasto platter.

mushroom and spinach salad with quick pesto dressing

serves 4 as a side dish

4 large **portabello** or **field mushrooms**

30 g (1 oz) **butter**, melted

1 tablespoon snipped **garlic chives**

4 slices **prosciutto**

75 g (2¹/2 oz) **baby English spinach leaves**

1 tablespoon **toasted pine nuts**

25 g (1 oz/1/4 cup) shaved **parmesan cheese**

1 tablespoon ready-made **pesto**

2 tablespoons **olive oil**

2 teaspoons **cider vinegar**

Heat the grill (broiler) to high. Trim the stems from the mushrooms and place the caps on the grill tray, gill-side-down. Grill for about 4 minutes, or until softened slightly. Mix together the butter and chives, then turn the mushrooms over and brush the chive butter all over the gills. Grill for another 4 minutes, or until soft. Remove the mushrooms from the heat, cut them into quarters and keep warm.

Put the prosciutto on the grill tray and cook for about 4 minutes, or until crisp, then break into several pieces.

Arrange the spinach on a serving plate and top with the warm mushroom quarters, prosciutto, pine nuts and parmesan. Put the pesto, oil and vinegar in a small screw-top jar, shake well to combine and season with salt and pepper. Drizzle over the salad and serve immediately.

side salad of grilled mixed vegetables

serves 4 as a side dish

1 **red capsicum (pepper)**

1 **yellow capsicum (pepper)**

2 **zucchini (courgettes)**, halved

4 **button mushrooms**, quartered

1 **onion**, cut into wedges

140 g (5 oz) **jap (kent) pumpkin**, cut into 4 thin slices

4 **garlic cloves**

2 tablespoons ready-made **pesto**

2 tablespoons **extra virgin olive oil**

35 g (1 1/4 oz/1/3 cup) shaved **parmesan cheese**

Heat the grill (broiler) to high. Cut the capsicums into large flat pieces and remove the seeds and membranes. Cook, skin-side-up, under the hot grill until the skin blackens and blisters. Leave to cool in a plastic bag.

While the capsicum is cooling, spread the zucchini, mushroom, onion and pumpkin on the grill tray and grill for 12 minutes, or until cooked. Remove from the grill and allow to cool.

Peel the skin from the cooled capsicum and gently toss the flesh in a large serving bowl with all the other grilled vegetables. In a small bowl, mix together the pesto and oil. Season to taste with salt and freshly ground pepper and drizzle over the vegetables. Gently toss together, scatter with the parmesan and serve.

bacon and potato skewers with tarragon cream

makes 8

16 **new potatoes**
8 slices **bacon**, rind removed
olive oil, for brushing

tarragon cream
125 g (4 oz/1/2 cup) **whole-egg mayonnaise**
3 **anchovy fillets**, finely chopped
1/2 teaspoon **Dijon mustard**
1 tablespoon chopped **tarragon leaves**

Soak eight bamboo skewers in cold water for 30 minutes. While the skewers are soaking, put the potatoes in a saucepan of cold, lightly salted water. Bring to the boil, then reduce the heat and simmer for about 10 minutes, or until tender when pierced with a sharp knife. Drain well and leave to cool, then cut the potatoes in half lengthways.

Heat the grill (broiler) to high. Cut the bacon widthways into four strips. Wrap a piece of bacon around each potato half and thread 4 pieces onto each skewer. Brush the bacon and potatoes with a little oil and grill for 3–4 minutes, then turn the skewers and grill for another 3–4 minutes, or until the potatoes and bacon are browned on both sides and the bacon is cooked through.

Put the tarragon cream ingredients in a small bowl and stir in about 1 tablespoon of hot water. Mix together well. Drizzle over the skewers and serve warm.

asparagus with parmesan and sumac

serves 4 as a side dish

350 g (12 oz/2 bunches) **asparagus**, trimmed

2 tablespoons **virgin olive oil**

40 g (1¹/2 oz) **butter**

2 **garlic cloves**, crushed

1 teaspoon **sumac**, optional (see tip)

4 **Roma (plum) tomatoes**, peeled, seeded and chopped

2 tablespoons snipped **chives**

50 g (1³/4 oz/¹/2 cup) freshly grated **parmesan cheese**

Heat the grill (broiler) to very hot. Bring a saucepan of lightly salted water to the boil, add the asparagus spears and blanch for 1 minute. Drain well, refresh under cold water and pat dry with paper towels.

Put the oil in a large, shallow ovenproof dish, add the asparagus spears and roll them around in the oil. Place the dish under the grill and cook the asparagus for 3–4 minutes, or until tender, turning once.

Meanwhile, melt the butter in a saucepan. Add the garlic and sumac and cook over medium heat for 1 minute, or until fragrant. Remove from the heat, stir in the tomato and chives and season to taste. Spoon the mixture over the asparagus, scatter with the parmesan and grill for another 3 minutes, or until the cheese has melted. Serve immediately.

tip Sumac is a purple-red spice with a mild lemony flavour available from Middle Eastern grocery stores and gourmet food shops. If you can't obtain any, you could use ¹/2 teaspoon sweet paprika in this recipe instead.

151

roasted rosemary potatoes with red capsicum aïoli

serves 4 as a side dish

300 g (10¹/2 oz) **baby new potatoes,** halved

2 tablespoons **oil**

2 tablespoons **rosemary leaves**

red capsicum aïoli

1 large **red capsicum (pepper)**

1 **garlic clove,** crushed

1 large **egg yolk**

1–1¹/2 tablespoons **lemon juice**

125 ml (4 fl oz/¹/2 cup) **extra virgin olive oil**

Preheat the oven to 190°C (375°F/Gas 5). Put the potatoes in a roasting tin with the oil and rosemary. Toss to coat and season with salt. Roast for 20–30 minutes, or until the potatoes are golden and crispy.

Meanwhile, heat the grill (broiler) to high. Cut the capsicum into large flat pieces and remove the seeds and membranes. Grill, skin-side-up, until the skin blackens and blisters. Leave to cool in a plastic bag, then peel away the skin and roughly chop the flesh.

To make the aïoli, blend the garlic, egg yolk and 1 tablespoon of the lemon juice in a blender. With the motor running, slowly add the oil in a thin stream until the sauce thickens (if you add the oil too quickly the aïoli may not thicken). Add the grilled capsicum and blend until smooth. Season with salt and pepper to taste, and add a little extra lemon juice if you think it needs it. Serve the aïoli as a dipping sauce with the roasted potatoes.

tip This aïoli is also delicious drizzled over chargrilled vegetables and meat.

eggplant stacks

serves 4 as a side dish

1 small **eggplant (aubergine)**, cut into 4 thick slices

oil, for brushing

2 **vine-ripened tomatoes**, quartered

150 g (5 1/2 oz) **rocket (arugula) leaves**

150 g (5 1/2 oz) **bocconcini (fresh baby mozzarella) cheese**, sliced

4 tablespoons **virgin olive oil**

1 tablespoon **white wine vinegar**

1 **garlic clove**, crushed

6 **kalamata olives**, pitted and finely chopped

2 tablespoons finely chopped **basil leaves**

Heat the grill (broiler) to high. Brush the eggplant slices generously with oil. Place on the grill tray, season with salt and pepper and grill for about 10 minutes, or until lightly browned and almost cooked through, turning once during cooking.

Add the tomato to the grill tray, lightly brush with oil and season with salt and freshly ground pepper. Grill for another 2 minutes, then remove the tomato and eggplant from the heat and leave to cool.

To assemble the stacks, arrange the rocket leaves on four serving plates. Add an eggplant slice, and top each with some tomato and bocconcini.

In a small bowl, whisk together the oil, vinegar and garlic. Add the olives and season to taste. Spoon over the stacks, sprinkle with the basil and serve warm.

over the grill

fire up the hotplate

In over-the-grill cooking, the grill is heated from underneath. The most celebrated form of this style of cooking is of course the outdoor barbecue, where everyone can smell the delicious aroma of food sizzling on a hotplate for miles around. Barbecues can be fired by gas, electricity, wood, coals or briquettes and come in many different types and sizes, including braziers, Hibachis and other portable barbecues, open barbecues, and covered or kettle barbecues. Back in the kitchen, portable grills, griddles and chargrill pans give the effect and the seared, smoky taste of meats and vegetables cooked on an outdoor barbecue. They are especially good for smaller gatherings and informal light meals and lunches such as toasted sandwiches and foccacias. Portable grilling pans are not only versatile, but are also simple to clean.

sizzling hot tips

Read the manufacturer's instructions before using a barbecue for the first time. Never leave a lit barbecue unattended — have all your food and utensils ready and close at hand before you start cooking, and keep a fire extinguisher nearby in case of emergency. Never use an oil spray near a lit barbecue as the oil may ignite, and always remember to completely extinguish a fire once you have finished cooking on it.

To stop food sticking to the hotplate, brush the food with oil (rather than the barbecue) just before cooking, make sure the hotplate is at the right temperature, and don't turn the food until the surface has cooked and released itself naturally from the grill. Sear meat over high heat for a few minutes to seal it all over, then move it away slightly from the high heat to let it finish cooking through.

Foil, paperbark, banana leaves and corn husks make excellent non-edible wrappers to help stop food drying out on a hot grill. Edible wrappers include tortillas and vine leaves (see pages 162–163).

is it ready yet?

Touch is a good way to estimate whether a steak is cooked to your liking — never pierce a plump piece of steak with a fork as this will let the precious juices escape. Instead, lightly press the meat with a pair of tongs. With a little practice you'll find that when you press rare meat with tongs it will be soft to touch, whereas medium-cooked meat offers a little resistance, and well-done meat will be firm to touch. The actual cooking time will depend on the thickness of the steak and the heat of the hotplate. To test if chicken or pork are cooked, pierce the thickest part with a skewer: the juices should run clear. If there is any sign of blood, cook the meat a little longer. Test fish by gently flaking the flesh in the thickest part with a fork: it should be white and opaque, but still moist.

grill it

the perfect steak

Bring the steak to **room temperature** and **brush** with oil to stop it sticking to the hotplate.

When the hotplate is **completely** hot, put the steak on and **leave** until ready to turn.

When **grill marks** appear underneath, **turn** the steak with tongs — try not to squeeze, prod or poke the steak so it stays juicy.

A medium-cooked steak is **firm** to touch and **pink** in the middle, with crisp brown edges. **Rest** before serving for a **tender**, juicy result.

wonderful wrappers

Banana leaves are perfect for Asian-style dishes. They should be blanched first and are **not edible**.

Fresh **vine leaves** need to be quickly blanched first to **soften** them. They taste **delicious**.

Corn husks are highly attractive wrappers. First **soak** them in water for 1 hour so they don't scorch.

Corn or flour **tortillas** are **great** for pre-cooked fillings and only need a light grilling to **heat** through.

grilling with skewers

Soak wooden skewers in cold water for at least **30 minutes** before cooking so they don't scorch.

Taking care not to **crowd** the grill, put the skewers on the **hot** grill tray. **Turn** halfway during cooking.

Baste the skewers during cooking so the food stays lovely and **moist**. Handle the food as little as possible.

To **release** the cooked food, **gently twist** it first to loosen before pulling it off the skewer.

zucchini wrapped in prosciutto

makes 4

2 small **green zucchini (courgettes)**
2 small **yellow zucchini (courgettes)**
8 thin slices **prosciutto**

sage butter
40 g (1 1/2 oz) **butter**, softened
1 tablespoon finely chopped **sage leaves**
1 tablespoon finely chopped **semi-dried (sun-blushed) tomatoes**

Preheat a barbecue flat plate to low. Meanwhile, bring a large saucepan of water to the boil. Add the whole zucchini, then reduce the heat and simmer for 5 minutes, or until almost tender. Drain well, allow to cool, then pat dry with paper towels.

To make the sage butter, put the butter, sage and tomato in a small bowl and mix well. Season to taste with salt and pepper and set aside until needed.

Wrap 2 slices of prosciutto around each zucchini — it should stick together quite easily. Put the zucchini on the hotplate and cook for about 15 minutes, or until cooked through, turning halfway through cooking and keeping a close watch to ensure they don't burn. Serve hot, with a dollop of sage butter.

barbecued corn cakes

makes 12

125 g (4 1/2 oz/1 cup) **plain (all-purpose) flour**

75 g (2 1/2 oz/1/2 cup) **fine polenta**

1 teaspoon **baking powder**

1 teaspoon **salt**

1 **egg**

170 ml (5 1/2 oz/2/3 cup) **buttermilk**

1 cooked **corn cob**, kernels cut off

1 tablespoon chopped **pickled jalapeño chilli**

1 large **red chilli**, seeded and chopped

1 tablespoon chopped **coriander (cilantro) leaves**

1 tablespoon chopped **parsley**

olive oil, for brushing

tomato and avocado relish

4 **Roma (plum) tomatoes**, quartered

1 tablespoon **lime juice**

1 **avocado**, cut into 2 cm (3/4 inch) cubes

Preheat a barbecue grill plate or flat plate to medium. Put the flour, polenta, baking powder and salt in a large bowl, making a well in the centre. In a small bowl, whisk together the egg and buttermilk, then pour into the flour mixture and stir to thoroughly combine. Mix through the corn, chillies, coriander and parsley.

Brush the barbecue hotplate with 1 tablespoon of oil. Cook the tomato quarters for 2 minutes on each side, then remove and allow to cool. To make the tomato and avocado relish, roughly chop the cooled tomato and place in a bowl with the lime juice and 1/2 teaspoon salt. Add the avocado cubes, mix gently and set aside.

Brush the hotplate with another tablespoon of oil. Spoon 2 tablespoons of the corn cake batter onto the hotplate to form a round cake, then repeat until the batter is used up — you should have enough to make 12 corn cakes. Cook for 2 minutes, or until bubbles appear on the surface. Turn and cook for a further 2–3 minutes, or until golden brown, brushing the hotplate with more oil if necessary. Serve the corn cakes hot, with the tomato and avocado relish on the side.

tip For a great finger food idea, cook teaspoons of the mixture into tiny corn cakes and top with a little sour cream and a coriander (cilantro) leaf.

chargrilled chicken and pink grapefruit salad

serves 4 as a starter

4 x 200 g (7 oz) **chicken breast fillets**

4 tablespoons **virgin olive oil**

2 teaspoons **balsamic vinegar**

2 **pink grapefruit**

1/2 teaspoon **Dijon mustard**

11/2 tablespoons **pickled pink peppercorns**, drained and rinsed

1 tablespoon snipped **chives**

rocket (arugula) leaves, to serve

Place the chicken breasts between two sheets of plastic wrap and pound each one with a mallet or rolling pin until 1.5 cm (5/8 inch) thick. Put 2 tablespoons of the oil in a shallow dish with the vinegar, and season with salt and freshly ground pepper. Add the chicken breasts, swish them around to coat, then cover and marinate in the refrigerator for 15 minutes, turning once.

Preheat a barbecue grill plate to medium and brush lightly with oil. Drain the chicken and cook on the hotplate for 7–8 minutes, or until cooked through, turning once. Remove from the heat, allow to cool to room temperature, then cut the chicken into slices about 1 cm (1/2 inch) thick.

Peel the grapefruit, removing all the bitter white pith. Working over a bowl to catch the juices, cut the grapefruit into segments between the membrane, removing any seeds. Reserve 1 tablespoon of the captured grapefruit juice and whisk in the mustard and remaining oil to make a dressing. Add the peppercorns and chives and season to taste with salt and freshly ground pepper.

Arrange the rocket leaves on four serving plates and top with the chicken and grapefruit segments. Drizzle with the dressing and serve.

algerian sardine patties

makes 6

450 g (1 lb) **fresh sardines**, gutted

1 slice **white bread**

1 large **garlic clove,** crushed

2 tablespoons chopped **parsley**

pinch of **cumin seeds**

pinch of **paprika**

2 large **eggs**, lightly beaten

4 tablespoons **plain (all-purpose) flour**, plus extra, for dusting

oil, for brushing

lemon wedges, to serve

Using a sharp knife, slice each sardine up along the middle into two neat fillets, and scrape the flesh away from the skins. Using tweezers, remove as many bones as possible, then roughly chop the sardines and place in a bowl.

Put the bread in a food processor and blend into fine breadcrumbs, or chop finely by hand. Add to the fish with the garlic, parsley, cumin, paprika, egg, flour and a little salt, and mix together well. With lightly floured hands, form the mixture into six balls and sit them on a plate. Cover and refrigerate for 30 minutes.

Preheat a barbecue grill plate or flat plate to medium. Brush the hotplate with a little oil, then add the fish balls and flatten them out slightly into a pattie shape. Cook for 4–5 minutes on each side, or until golden brown and cooked through. Serve at once with the lemon wedges.

tip You could also make these patties from herrings or mackerel.

zucchini, provolone and capsicum bruschetta

serves 4 as a starter

2 small **yellow capsicums (peppers)**

2 **zucchini (courgettes)**

oil, for brushing

3 tablespoons torn **purple basil leaves**

50 g (13/4 oz) shaved or very thinly sliced **provolone cheese**

1 **garlic clove**, crushed

11/2 tablespoons **extra virgin olive oil**

4 x 2.5 cm (1 inch) thick slices **ciabatta** or other **Italian-style bread**

2 **garlic cloves**, halved

Preheat a barbecue grill plate to medium. Cut each capsicum into four flat pieces and remove the seeds and membranes. Place skin-side-down on the hotplate and grill for about 8 minutes, or until the skins blacken and blister. Leave to cool in a plastic bag for about 5 minutes, then peel away the skin, slice the flesh into two long strips and put them in a bowl.

Slice the zucchini lengthways into 5 mm (1/4 inch) ribbons and brush both sides with oil. Put them on the hotplate and sprinkle lightly with salt. Cook for 2–3 minutes on each side, or until the slices turn soft and light brown grill lines form on both sides. Add to the capsicum strips along with the basil.

Slice the provolone into similar-sized strips as the capsicum and add them to the grilled vegetables. Combine the crushed garlic and extra virgin olive oil and season to taste. Drizzle over the grilled vegetables and toss lightly.

Put the ciabatta slices on a clean section of the barbecue and cook for 1 minute, or until grill lines form. Rotate the slices at right angles and grill for another minute to give a crisscross chargrill pattern underneath. Turn the slices over and repeat on the other side. Rub half a cut garlic clove over both sides of each slice of toasted bread. Transfer to a serving plate and top with a loose pile of the grilled vegetable mixture. Serve warm, or at room temperature.

Cook the zucchini slices on
the **hotplate** until
grill lines form.

Rub **half** a cut garlic clove
over **both sides** of
each slice of toasted bread.

scallops with lime and ginger butter

serves 4 as a starter

75 g (2¹/₂ oz) **unsalted butter**
6 **makrut (kaffir lime) leaves**, finely chopped
1 teaspoon finely grated fresh **ginger**
1 teaspoon finely chopped **lemon grass**, white part only
1 teaspoon **fish sauce**
16 cleaned **scallops**, on the half-shell

Preheat a barbecue flat plate or grill plate to medium. Melt the butter in a small saucepan on the stovetop over low heat. Remove from the heat and stir in the makrut leaves, ginger, lemon grass and fish sauce. Cover and keep warm.

Remove the scallops from their shells — you may need to use a small, sharp knife to slice them free, being careful not to leave any scallop meat behind. Rinse the scallops, pat them dry with paper towels and place in a bowl with half the butter mixture. Mix gently to coat the scallops.

Wipe the scallop shells with a clean, damp cloth and put them on the edge of the barbecue to warm through. When warm, arrange the shells on four serving plates.

Sear the scallops on the hotplate for 40–60 seconds on each side, or until golden and just cooked through. Quickly transfer to the warm shells and drizzle with the remaining butter mixture. Serve immediately.

tip Never soak scallops in water as they act like sponges and absorb water, and will tend to stew rather than brown during cooking.

chicken in pandanus leaves

makes 20

2 **garlic cloves**, crushed

2 cm (3/4 inch) piece fresh **ginger**,
   peeled and chopped

1 small **onion**, chopped

1 stem **lemon grass**, white part
   only, sliced

1 tablespoon **fish sauce**

2 tablespoons **kecap manis**

1 tablespoon **Worcestershire sauce**

125 ml (4 fl oz/1/2 cup) **coconut milk**

2 teaspoons grated **palm sugar** or
   soft brown sugar

500 g (1 lb 2 oz) **chicken thigh fillets**,
   cut into 20 large chunks

20 **pandanus leaves** (see tip)

dipping sauce

125 ml (4 fl oz/1/2 cup) **white vinegar**

3 tablespoons shaved **palm sugar**
   or **soft brown sugar**

1 tablespoon **dark soy sauce**

1 teaspoon **toasted sesame seeds**

Put the garlic, ginger, onion, lemon grass, fish sauce, kecap manis, Worcestershire sauce and 1/4 teaspoon of pepper in a food processor and blend to a smooth paste. Gradually blend in the coconut milk and sugar.

Transfer the paste to a shallow non-metallic dish, add the chicken and mix together well. Cover with plastic wrap and refrigerate for 2 hours. Put the dipping sauce ingredients in a bowl and stir until the sugar has dissolved. Set aside until needed.

Preheat a barbecue grill plate or flat plate to medium. Trim the pandanus leaves into strips about 15 cm (6 inches) long. Put a piece of chicken on each leaf, then roll each one up tightly and secure with a toothpick to make 20 parcels.

Put the parcels on a lightly oiled hotplate and cook for 5–6 minutes on each side, or until the chicken is cooked through. Serve hot with the dipping sauce.

tip Fresh pandanus leaves are available from Asian grocery stores. They impart a floral flavour to cooked dishes but are not edible.

moroccan stuffed sardines

serves 4 as a starter

couscous stuffing

75 g (2¹/2 oz) **couscous**

2 tablespoons **olive oil**

2 tablespoons finely chopped
   dried apricots

3 tablespoons **raisins**

1 tablespoon **flaked toasted almonds**

1 tablespoon chopped **parsley**

1 tablespoon chopped **mint**

grated **zest** of 1 **orange**

2 tablespoons **orange juice**

1 teaspoon finely chopped **preserved
   lemon rind**

1 teaspoon **ground cinnamon**

¹/2 teaspoon **harissa**

16 large **fresh** or **preserved vine leaves**

16 large fresh **sardines**, butterflied

oil, for brushing

lemon wedges, to serve

400 g (14 oz) **thick plain yoghurt**

Start by making the couscous stuffing. Put the couscous in a bowl and add half the oil and 50 ml (1³/4 fl oz) of boiling water. Stir and leave for 10 minutes to allow the couscous to absorb the liquid. Fluff up the couscous grains with a fork and add the remaining oil and stuffing ingredients. Season to taste and mix well.

Preheat a barbecue flat plate to medium. If you are using fresh vine leaves, bring a saucepan of water to the boil and blanch the leaves in batches for 30 seconds, then remove and pat dry on paper towels. If you are using preserved vine leaves, simply rinse and pat them dry.

Divide the couscous stuffing between the sardines, saving any leftover couscous for serving time. Fold the sardine fillets back together to enclose the stuffing. Gently wrap a vine leaf around each sardine and secure with a toothpick.

Lightly brush the hotplate with oil and cook the sardines for 6 minutes, turning halfway through cooking. Serve hot with lemon wedges, a dollop of yoghurt and any remaining couscous.

grill it

chorizo and haloumi skewers

makes 12

2 **chorizo sausages** (see tip)

2 x 180 g (6 oz) packets **haloumi cheese**

1 **lemon**

lemon and mint dressing

1 tablespoon **lemon juice**

2 tablespoons **extra virgin olive oil**

1 tablespoon finely chopped **mint**

1/2 teaspoon finely grated **lemon zest**

Soak 12 bamboo skewers in cold water for 30 minutes. Preheat a barbecue grill plate or flat plate to medium.

Chop the chorizo and haloumi into bite-sized pieces. Cut the lemon into 12 wedges, then slice each wedge in half. Thread the chorizo, haloumi and lemon pieces alternately onto the soaked bamboo skewers.

In a small bowl, whisk all the lemon and mint dressing ingredients together, then season to taste and set aside.

Brush the hotplate with a little oil, add the skewers and cook for a few minutes on each side, or until the chorizo is cooked through and the skewers are golden brown all over. Spoon the dressing over the hot skewers and serve at once.

tip Chorizo sausages are made from highly seasoned minced (ground) pork and are flavoured with garlic, chilli and a number of other spices. They are available from delicatessens, specialty butchers and some supermarkets.

warm asparagus with a creamy lemon-pepper dressing

serves 4 as a starter

4 tablespoons **extra virgin olive oil**

2 tablespoons **lemon juice**

3 tablespoons **crème fraîche**, softened

20 **asparagus spears**

Preheat a barbecue grill plate or flat plate to medium. In a small bowl, combine the oil and lemon juice, and season well with salt and freshly ground black pepper. Pour half the mixture into a shallow dish for coating the asparagus. Stir the crème fraîche through the remaining mixture, then season to taste and set aside.

Snap off and discard the tough ends from the asparagus spears. Put the spears in the shallow dish with the oil and lemon juice mixture and roll them around to coat.

Cook the asparagus on the hotplate, turning frequently with tongs, for about 4–5 minutes, or until just tender and lightly charred. If any spears begin to brown too quickly, move them to the outside of the barbecue.

Put the asparagus on a serving platter and pour the reserved crème fraîche dressing over the spears. Serve immediately.

cauliflower filo rolls

makes 8

300 g (10 1/2 oz) head of **cauliflower**

2 teaspoons **sesame seeds**

2 tablespoons **thick plain yoghurt**

1 tablespoon **toasted pine nuts**

50 g (1 3/4 oz/1/2 cup) grated **cheddar cheese**

1/2 teaspoon **ground cumin**

8 sheets **filo pastry**

50 g (1 3/4 oz) **butter**, melted

To toast sesame seeds, put them in a hot, non-stick frying pan and **dry-fry** until **golden**.

Fold the bottom edge of the pastry over the filling, then fold in the sides and **roll up** firmly.

Bring a large saucepan of water to the boil. Add the whole head of cauliflower and cook for 10 minutes, then drain well and allow to cool.

Meanwhile, put a non-stick frying pan over medium heat. When the pan is hot, add the sesame seeds and dry-fry for about 1–2 minutes, shaking the pan occasionally, until the seeds are golden and lightly toasted all over. Watch them carefully as they burn quite easily. Remove from the heat and leave to cool.

Preheat a barbecue flat plate to medium. Chop the cooled cauliflower into small pieces and place in a large bowl with the yoghurt, pine nuts, cheese, cumin, half the toasted sesame seeds and a little salt and pepper. Stir well to combine.

Lay one sheet of filo pastry, with the narrow end nearest you, on a flat surface and brush with melted butter to lightly coat. Put 2 tablespoons of the cauliflower mixture on the pastry, 10 cm (4 inches) from the edge nearest you, to form a narrow log of filling 10 cm (4 inches) long. Fold the bottom edge of the pastry up and over to enclose the filling. Roll in the sides and continue rolling firmly to form a spring roll. Repeat with the remaining pastry and filling to make eight rolls.

Cook the rolls on the hotplate for 3–4 minutes, turning them at frequent intervals so they cook on all sides. Sprinkle with the remaining sesame seeds and serve.

tip These rolls are delicious served as part of an antipasto platter, with your favourite yoghurt-based dip.

thai-style chicken cakes

makes 12

750 g (1 lb 10 oz) **minced (ground) chicken**

1 small **red onion**, diced

3 large **garlic cloves**, crushed

2 teaspoons finely grated fresh **ginger**

1 stem **lemon grass**, white part only, finely chopped

2 tablespoons **sweet chilli sauce**, plus extra, to serve

1 tablespoon **fish sauce**

4 tablespoons finely chopped **coriander (cilantro) leaves**

4 **makrut (kaffir lime) leaves**, finely chopped (see tip)

lime wedges, to serve

sweet chilli dipping sauce, to serve

Preheat a barbecue grill plate or flat plate to medium. Meanwhile, put the chicken, onion, garlic, ginger, lemon grass, sweet chilli sauce, fish sauce, coriander and makrut leaves in a bowl and mix well until thoroughly combined. Divide the mixture into 12 portions and shape into small, evenly sized patties.

Cook the patties on a lightly oiled hotplate for 2–3 minutes on each side, or until cooked through. Serve hot with lime wedges and a sweet chilli dipping sauce.

tip To keep any leftover makrut leaves fresh, store them in a plastic bag in the freezer.

グ

smoked mozzarella sandwiches

serves 4

8 thick slices **ciabatta** or other Italian-style bread
butter, for spreading
12 thin slices **smoked mozzarella cheese** (see tip)
2 **vine-ripened tomatoes**, thinly sliced
8 large **basil leaves**

Preheat a barbecue flat plate or grill plate to medium. Spread each slice of bread with butter, then place 4 slices, buttered-side-down, on a clean, flat surface. Layer the cheese, tomato and basil on top, then add the remaining bread slices, placing them buttered-side-up. Tie the sandwiches together with kitchen string.

Put the sandwiches on the hotplate, pressing them down firmly with a spatula. Grill for 3 minutes, pressing down firmly during cooking. Turn and cook the sandwiches for another 2 minutes, again pressing down firmly with the spatula, until the bread is golden brown and the filling has heated through.

Remove from the heat and cut each sandwich crossways into three 'fingers'. Arrange on four serving plates and serve hot, sprinkled with sea salt.

tip You can generally buy smoked mozzarella cheese at delicatessens or speciality cheese stores.

warm mediterranean lamb salad

serves 4

500 g (1 lb 2 oz) **lamb backstraps**
  or **loin fillets**
125 ml (4 fl oz/1/2 cup) **olive oil**
2 **garlic cloves**, crushed
2 teaspoons **thyme leaves**
1 teaspoon **ground black pepper**
3 small **red capsicums (peppers)**
5 **slender eggplants (aubergines)**,
  thickly sliced on the diagonal
2 tablespoons **olive tapenade**
100 g (31/2 oz) **semi-dried**
  (sun-blushed) tomatoes, sliced

1 **Lebanese (short) cucumber**, seeded
  and chopped
150 g (51/2 oz) **green beans**, trimmed
  and blanched
150 g (51/2 oz) **Niçoise** or **Ligurian olives**
100 g (31/2 oz) **baby rocket (arugula)**
  leaves

dressing
2 **garlic cloves**, crushed
2 tablespoons **extra virgin olive oil**
1 tablespoon **lemon juice**

Put the lamb in a non-metallic bowl. Combine half the oil with the garlic, thyme and pepper, then pour over the lamb and toss to coat. Set aside.

Heat the grill (broiler) to high. Cut the capsicums into large flat pieces, discarding the seeds and membrane. Arrange skin-side-up on the grill tray and grill until the skin blackens and blisters. Leave to cool in a plastic bag, then peel away the skin and cut the flesh into thirds.

Meanwhile, preheat a barbecue chargrill plate or chargrill pan to high. Toss the eggplant in the remaining oil to coat, then grill for 2–3 minutes on each side, or until golden. Remove and drain on crumpled paper towels.

Cook the lamb on the hot chargrill plate or pan for about 4 minutes on each side for medium rare, or until done to your liking. Remove from the heat, cover loosely with foil and leave to rest for 5 minutes.

Thinly slice the lamb across the grain and toss in a large bowl with the capsicum, eggplant, tapenade, tomato, cucumber, beans and olives. Add the rocket. Put the dressing ingredients in a small screw-top jar and shake well. Pour over the lamb salad, season with salt and pepper and toss to combine. Serve immediately.

chargrilled vegetables with mint and feta pesto

serves 4–6

1 **fennel bulb**

12 **spring onions (scallions)**

150 g (5¹/2 oz) **green beans**, trimmed

4 small **zucchini (courgettes)**,
   quartered lengthways

2 tablespoons **olive oil**

mint and feta pesto

80 g (2³/4 oz/1 bunch) **mint**, leaves picked

100 g (3¹/2 oz) **feta cheese**, crumbled

1 tablespoon **lemon juice**

125 ml (4 fl oz/¹/2 cup) **extra virgin
   olive oil**

Trim the base of the fennel bulb, remove the outer layer and cut the bulb into quarters lengthways. Cut out and discard the inner core, then slice the fennel into long pieces. Trim the spring onions, leaving about 7 cm (2³/4 inches) of the green stem on top, and remove the outer layer from around the white base. Lay all the vegetables in a shallow non-metallic dish, drizzle with the oil and toss to coat.

Preheat a barbecue grill plate or chargrill pan to medium. Grill all the vegetables, turning occasionally, until tender and charred — the beans and spring onions should take about 5–7 minutes, the fennel may take up to 10 minutes. You may need to cook the vegetables separately if your grill isn't large enough to cook them all at once. Transfer to a serving platter and allow to cool slightly.

Meanwhile, make the mint and feta pesto. Put the mint, feta and lemon juice in a food processor and blend until roughly chopped. With the motor running, add the oil in a thin stream and blend until incorporated. Season with freshly ground black pepper.

Serve the vegetables hot or at room temperature, with the mint and feta pesto on the side, or dolloped over the top.

panini

serves 4

2 **red capsicums (peppers)**
12 thin slices **pancetta** (see tip)
olive oil, for brushing
1 **eggplant (aubergine)**, cut into 8 thick slices
8 slices **ciabatta** or other **Italian-style bread**
150 g (5¹/2 oz) shaved **provolone cheese**
20 **basil leaves**
60 g (2¹/4 oz) **baby rocket (arugula) leaves**

Heat the grill (broiler) to high. Cut the capsicums into large flat pieces, discarding the seeds and membrane. Arrange skin-side-up on the grill tray and grill until the skin blackens and blisters. Leave to cool in a plastic bag, then peel away the skin.

Put the pancetta under the hot grill and cook for 1 minute on each side, or until lightly grilled but not too crispy.

Preheat a barbecue grill plate to high. Brush both sides of each eggplant slice with oil and grill for 3–4 minutes on each side, or until golden. Remove and drain on crumpled paper towels if necessary.

To assemble the panini, lay 4 slices of bread on a clean, flat surface. Layer the cheese, eggplant, pancetta, basil, rocket and capsicum over the top, then season with salt and pepper. Put the other bread slices on top, pressing down firmly.

Brush the hotplate liberally with oil and grill the panini for 30–60 seconds on each side, or until golden and heated through, pressing them down with a spatula during cooking. Cut each panini in half and serve immediately.

tip Pancetta is Italian cured pork belly, which is available at delicatessens. If you can't obtain any, use prosciutto instead.

summer salad with marinated tofu steaks

serves 4

500 g (1 lb 2 oz) block **firm tofu**
2 tablespoons **balsamic vinegar**
1 tablespoon **olive oil**
1 **garlic clove**, crushed

summer salad

250 g (9 oz/1 punnet) **cherry tomatoes**, halved
1/2 **red onion**, thinly sliced
1 small **Lebanese (short) cucumber**, sliced
1 handful **basil leaves**, shredded
12 **pitted kalamata olives**, halved
2 teaspoons **balsamic vinegar**
2 teaspoons **extra virgin olive oil**

Cut the tofu horizontally into four thin steaks, or into four large cubes if you prefer. Place in a large, shallow non-metallic dish and drizzle with the vinegar and oil. Add the garlic and season well with salt and pepper. Use your fingers to rub the mixture evenly all over the tofu, then cover and refrigerate for at least 30 minutes, or up to 4 hours, turning occasionally.

Preheat a barbecue flat plate to moderately hot. When you're nearly ready to eat, make the salad. Put the tomato, onion, cucumber, basil, olives and vinegar in a bowl, drizzle with the oil and toss together gently. Season well.

Cook the tofu on the hotplate for 2 minutes on each side, or until golden. Transfer to four serving plates and pile the salad over the top. Serve immediately, perhaps with some crusty bread.

barbecued squid with salsa verde

serves 4

4 cleaned **squid tubes**

3 tablespoons **olive oil**

3 **garlic cloves**, crushed

150 g (5½ oz) **mixed lettuce leaves**

250 g (9 oz/1 punnet) **cherry tomatoes**, halved

salsa verde

2 large handfuls **flat-leaf (Italian) parsley**

2 tablespoons chopped **dill**

2 tablespoons **extra virgin olive oil**

2 tablespoons **olive oil**

1 tablespoon **Dijon mustard**

2 **garlic cloves**, crushed

1 tablespoon **red wine vinegar**

1 tablespoon **baby capers**, rinsed and drained

4 **anchovy fillets**, drained

Open out the squid tubes by cutting through one side so you have one large piece, the inside facing upwards. Pat dry with paper towels. Using a sharp knife, and being careful not to cut all the way through, score the flesh on the diagonal in a series of lines about 5 mm (¼ inch) apart, then do the same in the opposite direction to form a crisscross pattern. Cut the squid into 4 cm (1½ inch) pieces and put in a non-metallic bowl. Combine the oil and garlic and pour over the squid, tossing to coat well. Cover and marinate in the refrigerator for 30 minutes.

Put all the salsa verde ingredients in a food processor and blend until just combined. Set aside until ready to use.

Preheat a barbecue flat plate to high. Drain the squid and cook for 1–2 minutes, or until curled up and just cooked through. Put the squid in a bowl with the salsa verde and toss until well coated. Arrange the lettuce and tomatoes on four serving plates, top with the squid, then season and serve at once.

chickpea burgers

makes 6

chickpea patties

2 teaspoons **olive oil**

1 small **onion**, finely chopped

2 **garlic cloves**, crushed

2 x 400 g (14 oz) tins **chickpeas**, rinsed and drained

95 g (3 1/2 oz/1/2 cup) **cooked brown rice** (see tip)

50 g (1 3/4 oz/1/3 cup) **sun-dried tomatoes**, chopped

spicy yoghurt dressing

200 g (7 oz) **thick plain yoghurt**

1 **garlic clove**, crushed

1/4 teaspoon **ground cumin**

1/4 teaspoon **ground coriander**

1 **eggplant (aubergine)**, cut into 1 cm (1/2 inch) slices

olive oil, for brushing

1 large **red onion**, sliced into rings

2 large handfuls **rocket (arugula) leaves**

6 pieces **Turkish bread**

To make the chickpea patties, heat the oil in a frying pan and cook the onion over medium heat for 2 minutes, or until soft and lightly golden. Add the garlic and cook for 1 more minute, then remove from the heat and allow to cool slightly. Put the onion mixture in a food processor with the chickpeas, rice and sun-dried tomato. Using a pulse action, process in short bursts until the mixture is combined and the chickpeas are broken up, but not completely mushy, scraping the bowl down with a spatula a few times during processing. Season to taste, then shape the mixture into six patties about 8 cm (3¼ inches) in diameter. Place on a tray lined with plastic wrap, then cover and refrigerate for 1 hour.

Put all the spicy yoghurt dressing ingredients in a small bowl and mix together well. Refrigerate until needed.

Preheat a barbecue flat plate to moderately hot. Brush the eggplant slices lightly on each side with oil, and toss a little oil through the onion rings. Cook the eggplant and onion on the hotplate until tender and lightly golden — the eggplant will need about 3–4 minutes each side, the onion about 5 minutes. Transfer the vegetables to a plate and set aside.

Brush the top of the chickpea patties lightly with oil, then put them face-down on the hotplate and cook for 3 minutes. Brush the top of the patties with a little oil, then turn and cook for a further 3 minutes, or until golden. They may stick a little, so make sure you get your spatula well underneath before turning.

While the chickpea patties are cooking, arrange the rocket, barbecued eggplant and onion on the Turkish bread slices. Add the hot chickpea patties, dollop with some of the spicy yoghurt dressing and serve at once.

tip You will need to cook about 55 g (1¾ oz/¼ cup) of brown rice for this recipe. If you like your Turkish bread toasted, lightly grill the slices on both sides on the edge of the flat plate while the patties are cooking.

Put the sautéed onion and garlic in a **food processor** with chickpeas, rice and tomato.

Pulse in **short** bursts, until the chickpeas are broken up but **not mushy**.

chargrilled asparagus with fried eggs, olives and capers

serves 4

175 g (6 oz/1 bunch) **green asparagus**, halved lengthways

175 g (6 oz/1 bunch) **white asparagus**, halved lengthways

95 g (3 1/2 oz/1/2 cup) **Ligurian olives**

2 tablespoons **baby capers**, rinsed and drained

1 handful **oregano leaves**

4 **eggs**

25 g (1 oz/1/4 cup) good-quality **shaved parmesan cheese**

extra virgin olive oil, to serve

crusty bread, to serve

Preheat a barbecue grill plate to medium. Brush the hotplate lightly with oil and grill the green and white asparagus for 2–3 minutes, turning frequently with tongs — the white asparagus may take slightly longer to cook.

Meanwhile, put the olives, capers and oregano in a small bowl and mix together well. Divide the grilled asparagus between four serving plates and scatter the olive mixture over the top.

Lightly brush the hotplate with a little more oil and cook the eggs to your liking. Arrange the eggs on top of the asparagus, then scatter with the parmesan, sprinkle with freshly cracked black pepper and drizzle with extra virgin olive oil. Serve at once, with crusty bread.

lebanese wrap with chargrilled chicken

serves 4

3 large **chicken breast fillets**

1 tablespoon **olive oil**

4 **Lebanese bread** rounds

200 g (7 oz) ready-made **hummus**

200 g (7 oz) ready-made **beetroot dip**

200 g (7 oz) **thick plain yoghurt**

3 **garlic cloves**, crushed

4 tablespoons chopped **flat-leaf (Italian) parsley**

10 **cos (romaine) lettuce leaves**, shredded

1 small **red onion**, thinly sliced

3 **Roma (plum) tomatoes**, thinly sliced

Place the chicken breasts between two sheets of plastic wrap and slightly flatten them with a mallet or rolling pin.

Preheat a barbecue grill plate, chargrill plate or chargrill pan to medium. Lightly brush the hotplate with oil and grill the chicken for 4 minutes on each side, or until cooked through. Remove from the heat, allow to cool slightly, then slice thinly.

Lay the bread rounds on a flat surface and spread evenly with the hummus and the beetroot dip, leaving a 3 cm (1 1/4 inch) border. Top with the chicken and drizzle with the combined yoghurt and garlic.

Sprinkle the parsley, lettuce, onion and tomato lengthways along the centre of each round and roll up tightly, tucking in the ends. Wrap tightly in foil and grill the wraps on the hotplate for 1–2 minutes on each side, or until the bread is crispy, pressing down lightly with a spatula during grilling. Unwrap the foil, cut the wraps in half on the diagonal and serve hot.

caesar salad with grilled king prawns

serves 4

20 **raw king prawns (shrimp)**, peeled
and deveined, tails intact, butterflied

140 ml (5 fl oz) **olive oil**

2 large **garlic cloves**, crushed

1 tablespoon **lemon juice**

8 slices **sourdough bread**

8 slices **prosciutto**

2 **baby cos (romaine) lettuces**,
leaves separated

4 **hard-boiled eggs**, quartered

3 tablespoons shaved **parmesan cheese**

dressing

2 **egg yolks**

3 **garlic cloves**, crushed

4 **anchovy fillets**, drained
(reserve 1 teaspoon of the oil)

1 teaspoon **Dijon mustard**

1 teaspoon **Worcestershire sauce**

1 tablespoon **lemon juice**

125 ml (4 fl oz/1/2 cup) **olive oil**

1 tablespoon finely grated
parmesan cheese

Put the prawns in a non-metallic bowl. Combine 4 tablespoons of the oil with the garlic and lemon juice. Pour over the prawns, then cover and chill for 30 minutes.

Preheat the oven to 200°C (400°F/Gas 6). Cut the crusts off each slice of bread, then cut each slice into nine cubes. Toss in a bowl with the remaining oil until well coated. Spread the cubes on a baking tray and bake for 10 minutes, or until golden brown and crisp, turning once. Leave to cool, then break into smaller pieces.

To make the dressing, blend the egg yolks, garlic, anchovies, anchovy oil, mustard, Worcestershire sauce and lemon juice in a food processor until combined. With the motor running, slowly add the oil in a thin stream — it will gradually thicken and turn creamy. Add the parmesan, blend well and season to taste. Refrigerate until needed.

Preheat a barbecue chargrill plate to medium. Cook the prosciutto for 2 minutes on each side, or until crisp. Set aside. Drain the prawns from the marinade and grill them for 2 minutes on each side, or until just cooked through.

Put the lettuce in a large bowl, add the dressing and toss to coat. Gently mix the prawns, prosciutto, croutons and egg quarters through. Divide between four serving plates and scatter with the shaved parmesan. Season to taste and serve at once.

gourmet sausage sandwiches

makes 12

yoghurt and coriander dressing
3 tablespoons **thick plain yoghurt**
2 tablespoons finely chopped
   coriander (cilantro)
2 teaspoons **lemon juice**

mustard mayonnaise
3 tablespoons **whole-egg mayonnaise**
2 tablespoons **Dijon mustard**

wholegrain tomato sauce
3 tablespoons **tomato sauce**
2 tablespoons **wholegrain mustard**

4 **pork sausages**
4 **chicken sausages**
4 **beef sausages**
1 tablespoon **olive oil**
2 **red onions**, sliced
2 **red apples**, cored and thinly sliced
150 g (5½ oz) **mixed lettuce leaves**
12 **pocket pitta breads**, split at the top

First, prepare the dressings, which you can do a day ahead if you wish. Simply combine the ingredients for the yogurt and coriander dressing, mustard mayonnaise and wholegrain tomato sauce in separate small bowls. Cover and refrigerate until needed.

Preheat a barbecue grill plate or flat plate to medium. Fry the sausages for about 10 minutes, or until cooked through, turning during cooking. Keep warm.

Heat the oil on the barbecue flat plate. Cook the onion on one area of the hotplate and the apples on another for 5 minutes, or until they begin to soften and turn golden. Remove from the heat and set aside.

Put some lettuce leaves in each pitta bread pocket. Slice the pork sausages in half lengthways and divide among 4 pitta pockets; add some barbecued onion and all the apple and drizzle with mustard mayonnaise. Slice the chicken sausages in half and divide among 4 pitta pockets; add some barbecued onion and drizzle with the yoghurt and coriander dressing. Slice the beef sausages and divide among the remaining pitta pockets; add the remaining onion and drizzle with the wholegrain tomato sauce. Wrap in colourful napkins and serve.

vietnamese pork kebabs with chilli lime pickle

serves 4

2 x 400 g (14 oz) **pork fillets**,
  trimmed and cut into 36 chunks
6 **spring onions (scallions)**
2 **garlic cloves**, crushed
1 tablespoon **sugar**
2 tablespoons **fish sauce**
1/4 teaspoon **white pepper**
1 tablespoon **peanut oil**
350 g (12 oz) **dried flat rice noodles**
1 **baby cos (romaine) lettuce**,
  leaves separated

2 tablespoons **coriander (cilantro) leaves**

chilli lime pickle

125 g (41/2 oz/1/2 cup) **hot lime pickle**
125 g (41/2 oz/1/2 cup) **thick plain yoghurt**
1 **bird's eye chilli**, seeded and
  finely chopped
1 tablespoon chopped **coriander (cilantro) leaves**

Soak 12 bamboo skewers in cold water for 30 minutes.

Thread 3 pieces of pork onto each skewer and place in a shallow non-metallic dish. Finely chop 4 spring onions, put in a mortar and pestle with the garlic and sugar and grind to a coarse paste. Mix in the fish sauce, white pepper and oil. Pour over the pork kebabs, turning to coat on all sides. Cover and refrigerate for 1–2 hours.

While the pork is marinating, put all the chilli lime pickle ingredients in a food processor and blend until smooth. Refrigerate until needed.

Cook the noodles in a large saucepan of boiling water for 4–5 minutes, or until tender. Drain and place in a covered bowl at room temperature until needed.

Preheat a barbecue grill plate or flat plate to high. Add the pork kebabs and grill for 3–4 minutes on each side, or until the pork is cooked through.

Cut the remaining spring onions lengthways into fine strips. Line four serving plates with lettuce leaves and put a nest of noodles on top. Put 3 pork skewers on each plate and scatter with the spring onion strips and coriander leaves. Serve with a dollop of chilli lime pickle on the side.

rainbow trout with salmon roe butter

serves 4

4 **rainbow trout**, cleaned and scaled

1 large **lime** or **lemon**, finely sliced

12 **lemon thyme** sprigs

olive oil, for brushing

salmon roe butter

50 g (13/4 oz) **butter**, softened

1 teaspoon **lime** or **lemon juice**

1/2 teaspoon chopped **tarragon**

1/2 teaspoon snipped **chives**

1 tablespoon **salmon roe** (see tip)

Fill each **trout** cavity with the **citrus slices** and add some lemon thyme sprigs.

Mix the herbs through the beaten butter, then **gently fold** in the salmon roe.

Preheat a barbecue flat plate to medium. Rinse each trout in cold water and pat dry inside and out with paper towels. Fill each trout cavity with slices of lime or lemon, put 3 sprigs of lemon thyme in each and season with salt and freshly ground pepper.

Lightly brush the hotplate and the trout with oil. Barbecue the trout for about 4 minutes, then turn and grill for a further 4 minutes, or until cooked through.

While the trout are cooking, make the salmon roe butter. In a bowl, beat the butter until smooth and stir in the lime or lemon juice, tarragon and chives. Gently fold in the salmon roe and season with freshly ground pepper.

Arrange the trout on four serving plates. Put a generous dollop of the salmon roe butter on each trout and serve immediately.

tip Salmon roe is available at most seafood stores and is sold either in small jars or by weight.

barbecued steaks filled with bocconcini and semi-dried tomatoes

serves 6

6 **New York style (boneless sirloin) steaks**

200 g (7 oz) **semi-dried (sun-blushed) tomatoes**, chopped

200 g (7 oz) **bocconcini (fresh baby mozzarella) cheese**, chopped

2 **garlic cloves**, crushed

2 tablespoons finely chopped **flat-leaf (Italian) parsley**

oil, for brushing

Cut a slit along the side of each steak to form a pocket. Combine the tomato, bocconcini, garlic and parsley in a small bowl with a little salt and pepper. Fill each steak with the mixture and secure with toothpicks to hold the filling in.

Preheat a barbecue grill plate or chargrill pan to medium. Just before cooking, brush the steaks lightly with oil and season with salt and pepper. Grill the steaks for 3–4 minutes on each side for medium rare, or until cooked to your liking, turning only once. Remove the toothpicks and serve with vegetables or a salad.

tip You can fill the steaks ahead of time — simply keep them covered in the refrigerator. Bring them to room temperature just before you're ready to cook.

niçoise salad with fresh tuna

serves 4

dressing
6 **anchovy fillets**, drained
2 tablespoons **red wine vinegar**
1 large **garlic clove**, crushed
125 ml (4 fl oz/1/2 cup) **olive oil**

750 g (1 lb 10 oz) **new potatoes**
1 **cos (romaine) lettuce**, shredded
1 **Lebanese (short) cucumber**, cut into
1 cm (1/2 inch) slices on the diagonal

1/2 **red capsicum (pepper)**, thinly sliced
200 g (7 oz) **green beans**, trimmed
and blanched
2 **tomatoes**, each cut into 8 wedges
1 small **red onion**, cut into thin wedges
200 g (7 oz) **Niçoise** or **Ligurian olives**
21/2 handfuls **basil leaves**, torn
olive oil, for brushing
600 g (1 lb 5 oz) fresh **tuna steaks**
3 **hard-boiled eggs**, quartered

To make the dressing, put the anchovies, vinegar and garlic in a food processor and blend until the anchovies are finely chopped. With the motor running, slowly add the oil and blend until combined.

Bring a large saucepan of water to the boil. Add the potatoes and cook for about 10 minutes, or until tender. Drain well, allow to cool a little, then peel and cut into 1 cm (1/2 inch) slices. Put the potato in a large bowl with the lettuce, cucumber, capsicum, beans, tomato, onion, olives and basil. Pour the dressing over and gently toss until combined.

Preheat a barbecue grill plate or chargrill pan to high. Brush the hotplate with oil and cook the tuna for 2 minutes on each side — it should still be a little pink in the middle. Slice the tuna into 2 cm (3/4 inch) cubes.

Arrange the salad on four serving plates and top with the tuna and egg quarters. Season with salt and freshly ground black pepper and serve immediately.

herbed lamb cutlets with preserved lemon couscous

serves 4

2 tablespoons finely chopped **thyme leaves**

2 teaspoons **freshly ground black pepper**

12 **French-trimmed lamb cutlets**

3 tablespoons **virgin olive oil**

2 tablespoons **soy sauce**

2 **garlic cloves**, crushed

oil, for brushing

preserved lemon couscous

1 tablespoon **olive oil**

185 g (6$\frac{1}{2}$ oz/1 cup) **couscous**

2 tablespoons thinly sliced **preserved lemon rind**

Sprinkle the thyme and pepper onto a plate. Use the mixture to coat both sides of each lamb cutlet, pressing it in well.

In a shallow non-metallic dish, whisk the oil, soy sauce and garlic until combined. Add the lamb cutlets, then cover and refrigerate for 20 minutes, turning once.

Preheat a barbecue grill plate or chargrill pan until very hot. Meanwhile, make the preserved lemon couscous. Bring 375 ml (13 fl oz/1$\frac{1}{2}$ cups) of water to the boil in a saucepan. Add the oil, then stir in the couscous and preserved lemon. Remove from the heat, cover and leave for 5 minutes. Just before serving, fluff up the couscous with a fork.

Shake the excess marinade off the cutlets and set them slightly apart on the barbecue hotplate. Grill for 1–2 minutes on each side, or until cooked to your liking. Serve the cutlets hot, on a bed of preserved lemon couscous.

grilled marinated spatchcock with green olive gremolata

serves 4

4 **spatchcocks (poussin)**
125 ml (4 fl oz/1/2 cup) **olive oil**
4 **garlic cloves**, crushed
2 teaspoons finely grated **lemon zest**
3 tablespoons **lemon juice**
2 tablespoons finely chopped **flat-leaf (Italian) parsley**,
  plus extra to serve
lemon wedges, to serve

green olive gremolata
100 g (3 1/2 oz) **pitted green olives**, finely chopped
2 teaspoons grated **lemon zest**
2 **garlic cloves**, finely chopped

First, joint the spatchcocks. Twist each thigh at the thigh joint to separate them from the body. Put the birds breast-side-down on a cutting board and cut along the backbone from the neck to the tail end. Carefully scrape away the flesh on one side of the backbone, cutting into the birds to expose the rib cage. Repeat on the other side of the backbone, being careful not to pierce the breast skin, then remove the ribs and backbones. Scrape away the flesh from each thigh bone and cut away the bone at the joint.

In a small bowl, combine the oil, garlic, lemon zest, lemon juice and parsley. Put the spatchcock pieces in a shallow non-metallic dish, pour the dressing over and toss well to coat. Cover and refrigerate for 3 hours, or overnight if convenient, turning occasionally.

Nearer to serving time, make the gremolata. Put the olives, lemon zest and garlic in a small bowl, mix well, then cover and refrigerate until needed.

Heat a barbecue grill plate, flat plate or chargrill pan to high. Cook the spatchcock for 5 minutes on each side, or until cooked through. Serve at once, with the gremolata, extra parsley and some lemon wedges.

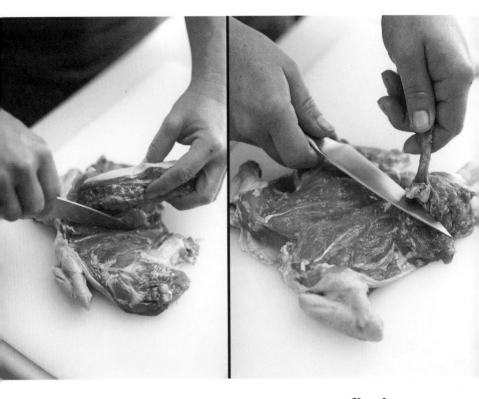

Using a sharp knife, **scrape away** the flesh on one side of the **backbone**.

Scrape away the **flesh** and carefully **cut away** the thigh **bone** at the joint.

chipolatas with sage and pancetta and fresh tomato salsa

serves 4

16 **chipolata sausages**
16 **sage leaves**
8 thin slices **pancetta**, cut in half
oil, for brushing

fresh tomato salsa
4 **Roma (plum) tomatoes**, cut into
1 cm (1/2 inch) cubes
1 tablespoon **extra virgin olive oil**
1 teaspoon **balsamic vinegar**
1 **garlic clove**, very thinly sliced
1 tablespoon chopped **mint leaves**
1 teaspoon chopped **sage leaves**

Soak eight bamboo skewers in cold water for 30 minutes. Meanwhile, put the chipolatas in a saucepan and cover with cold water. Bring to the boil, remove from the heat and drain well. (Parboiling the chipolatas will help them cook evenly.)

Preheat a barbecue grill plate or flat plate to low. Put a sage leaf along a chipolata and wrap half a slice of pancetta around it, to almost cover the chipolata. Repeat with the remaining sausages.

Thread 4 chipolatas onto a skewer about a quarter of the way in from one end of the sausages, so they poke out in the same direction like four little flags. Now push a second skewer up through the other end of the chipolatas so that they are suspended between two skewers. Repeat with the remaining sausages.

Lightly brush the hotplate with oil and cook the chipolatas for about 8 minutes, or until browned on both sides and cooked through, turning once — keep an eye on the pancetta to make sure it doesn't burn.

Meanwhile, put all the tomato salsa ingredients together in a bowl, season with salt and freshly ground black pepper and mix together well. Arrange the skewers on a serving plate, spoon some salsa over the top and serve at once.

marinated prawns with mango chilli salsa

serves 4–6

lemon dill marinade

4 tablespoons **lemon juice**

4 tablespoons **olive oil**

1 teaspoon **sea salt**

3 tablespoons chopped **dill**

1 kg (2 lb 4 oz) **raw prawns (shrimp)**, peeled and deveined, tails intact

150 g (5½ oz/1 bunch) **rocket (arugula)**

mango chilli salsa

450 g (1 lb/1½ cups) diced **fresh** or **tinned mango**

1 **red onion**, finely diced

1 small **red chilli**, seeded and finely chopped

1 tablespoon grated **lemon zest**

Put the lemon dill marinade ingredients in a large non-metallic bowl and mix well. Add the prawns, toss well, then cover and refrigerate for 1 hour.

Preheat the barbecue flat plate to moderately high. Just before you're ready to eat, put the mango chilli salsa ingredients in a bowl, mix well and set aside.

Drain the prawns from the marinade and cook them on the hotplate for about 2–4 minutes, turning once, or until they have changed colour but are still soft and fleshy to touch. Take them off the heat straight away and let them cool slightly.

Arrange a bed of rocket on individual serving plates. Add a generous scoop of salsa, then the prawns. Season to taste and serve at once.

rosemary and pepper rib-eye steaks with olive oil mash

serves 4

4 tablespoons roughly chopped **rosemary**

4 tablespoons **freshly ground black pepper**

250 ml (9 fl oz/1 cup) **olive oil**

4 **rib-eye steaks**

olive oil mash

750 g (1 lb 10 oz) **potatoes**

4 tablespoons **extra virgin olive oil**

1 **garlic clove**, chopped

125 ml (4 fl oz/1/2 cup) **cream (whipping)**, approximately

Combine the rosemary, pepper and oil in a large shallow non-metallic dish. Add the steaks, turn to coat well on both sides, then cover and refrigerate overnight.

Preheat a barbecue grill plate to medium. Meanwhile, boil, steam or microwave the potatoes until tender.

Drain the steaks and cook them on the hotplate for about 10 minutes on each side for medium rare, or until cooked to your liking — the exact cooking time will vary depending on the thickness of your steaks. Take them off the heat, cover loosely with foil and allow to rest for 5 minutes.

While the steaks are resting, make the olive oil mash. Drain the hot, cooked potatoes, then put them in a large bowl and mash them. Gently heat the oil and garlic in a small pan until the garlic starts to sizzle and soften. Take the pan off the heat and strain the oil, discarding the garlic. Meanwhile, heat the cream in another small pan until just hot. Gradually beat the warm garlic oil into the mashed potato and then add enough cream to give a soft texture. Season to taste with salt and cracked black pepper. Serve hot with the rib-eye steaks.

lamb murtabak with minted mango yoghurt

makes 8

pastry

375 g (13 oz/3 cups) **plain (all-purpose) flour**
75 g (2¹/2 oz/¹/3 cup) **ghee**
250 ml (9 fl oz/1 cup) **milk**

filling

2 tablespoons **ghee**
2 large **onions**, finely chopped
1 **celery stalk**, finely chopped
3 **garlic cloves**, finely chopped
1 tablespoon finely grated fresh **ginger**
2 tablespoons **Indian-style curry powder**
1 tablespoon **red chilli paste**
500 g (1 lb 2 oz) **minced (ground) lamb**
65 g (2³/4 oz/¹/2 cup) **frozen baby peas**, thawed
1 **egg**, lightly beaten
3 tablespoons **melted ghee**, for brushing

minted mango yoghurt

250 g (9 oz/1 cup) **thick plain yoghurt**
4 tablespoons **mango chutney**
1 large handful **mint leaves**, chopped
¹/4 teaspoon **salt**

Using a **rolling pin**, roll each pastry portion into a 25 cm (10 inch) **round**.

Spread the filling in the centre of the pastry and **fold** the sides towards the middle.

To make the pastry, put the flour and ghee in a food processor with a pinch of salt and blend until well combined. Add the milk and process until the mixture comes together. Turn the dough out onto an unfloured work surface and knead until smooth. Divide into eight equal portions, then place on a tray, cover with plastic wrap and allow to rest for several hours.

Meanwhile, make the filling. Heat the ghee in a large saucepan, then add the onion, celery, garlic and ginger and cook over medium heat, stirring occasionally, for 5–10 minutes, or until the onion is soft. Add the curry powder, chilli paste and lamb and mix well. Cook, stirring occasionally, for about 10 minutes, or until the lamb is cooked through. Stir in the peas, take the pan off the heat and allow the mixture to cool. Add the egg and mix until well combined.

Put the minted mango yoghurt ingredients in a bowl and mix well. Cover and refrigerate until needed.

Preheat a barbecue grill plate to low. Using a rolling pin, roll each dough portion into a 25 cm (10 inch) round. Brush with melted ghee and fold in half. Brush with a little more ghee and fold again into quarters. Now roll out the dough again into another 25 cm (10 inch) round. Place the round on a tray and cover with a sheet of baking paper. Repeat with the remaining dough portions, placing a sheet of baking paper between each round to stop them sticking together.

Spread one-eighth of the filling into the centre of a pastry round. Fold two opposite sides of the circle into the centre, overlapping them slightly. Fold over the remaining two sides to enclose the filling. Press down to form a flat square package. Repeat with the remaining dough and filling to make eight murtabak.

Lightly brush the hotplate with oil. Put the murtabak folded-side-down on the hotplate and cook for about 5–6 minutes on each side, or until the pastry is cooked through. Serve hot, with the minted mango yoghurt on the side.

veal stacks with mozzarella

serves 4

1 small **eggplant (aubergine)**

125 g (4¹/2 oz/¹/2 cup) **tomato passata (puréed tomatoes)**

1 **garlic clove**, crushed

¹/4 teaspoon **sugar**

oil, for brushing

4 x 150 g (5¹/2 oz) butterflied **veal loin steaks**

50 g (1³/4 oz) **baby rocket (arugula) leaves**

75 g (2¹/2 oz/¹/2 cup) coarsely grated **mozzarella cheese**

Slice the eggplant into 5 mm (¹/4 inch) thick rounds. Put them in a colander and sprinkle generously with salt to draw out the juice. Leave for 20 minutes, then rinse well under cold running water and pat dry with paper towels.

Put the passata, garlic and sugar in a small bowl. Season to taste and set aside.

Preheat a barbecue grill plate, flat plate or chargrill pan to high. Brush both sides of each eggplant slice with a little oil and cook for about 15 minutes, turning once, or until lightly browned on both sides. Remove from the heat.

Heat the grill (broiler) to high. Brush the veal steaks with a little oil, season with salt and pepper, then grill on the hotplate for about 3–5 minutes on each side, or until nicely browned and cooked to your liking. Remove from the heat.

Arrange the rocket, eggplant slices, passata mixture and mozzarella on top of each steak. Put the steaks on the grill plate under the hot grill and cook for 1 minute, or until the cheese is golden. Serve hot.

vine-wrapped blue-eye with dill and lemon butter

serves 4

8 **fresh** or **preserved vine leaves**

2 tablespoons chopped **dill**

60 g (2¼ oz) **butter**, softened

4 x 200 g (7 oz) **blue-eye fillets** (see tip)

1 tablespoon **lemon juice**

oil, for brushing

If you are using fresh vine leaves, bring a saucepan of water to the boil and blanch the leaves in batches for 30 seconds. Pat dry on crumpled paper towels. If you are using preserved vine leaves, simply rinse and dry them. Place 2 leaves on a work surface, slightly overlapping them. Repeat with the remaining leaves.

Combine the dill and butter in a small bowl and divide into four portions. Put each portion in the centre of each set of overlapping vine leaves. Rest a piece of fish on top of the butter and drizzle with the lemon juice. Season with salt and pepper. Wrap the fish in the vine leaves by bringing the edge closest to you over the fish, folding in the sides (if the leaves are wide enough) as you go, rolling up very firmly. Put the parcels on a plate, then cover and refrigerate for 30 minutes.

Preheat a barbecue flat plate to medium. Brush the hotplate with oil and grill the fish for 6–8 minutes, or until cooked through, turning once. Serve hot, with a Mediterranean-style salad.

tip Any thick fish fillet can be used in this recipe if blue-eye is unavailable.

mexican-style chicken with avocado salsa and cheese quesadillas

serves 4

avocado salsa

1 large **avocado**, diced

1 large **tomato**, seeded and diced

1/2 small **red onion**, diced

3 tablespoons finely chopped
    coriander (cilantro) leaves
    and **stems**

2 tablespoons **extra virgin olive oil**

1 tablespoon **lime juice**

3 teaspoons **sweet chilli sauce**

1 **garlic clove**, crushed

4 x 150 g (5 1/2 oz) **chicken breast fillets**

2 x 35 g (1 1/4 oz) packets **taco seasoning**

oil, for brushing

cheese quesadillas

200 g (7 oz) grated **cheddar cheese**

1 1/2 tablespoons finely chopped
    coriander (cilantro) leaves and **stems**

1 small **red chilli**, seeded and finely
    chopped

1 teaspoon **sea salt**

4 **flour tortillas**

Preheat a barbecue grill plate or chargrill pan to medium. Meanwhile, put all the avocado salsa ingredients in a small bowl, mix well and set aside.

Place the chicken breasts between two sheets of plastic wrap and slightly flatten them with a rolling pin or mallet. Put them in a bowl with the taco seasoning and toss well to coat, pressing the mixture in with your hands. Lightly brush the barbecue hotplate with oil, then cook the chicken for about 5 minutes on each side, or until golden and cooked through. Take the chicken off the heat and keep warm. Turn the barbecue up high.

To make the quesadillas, put the cheese, coriander, chilli and salt in a bowl and mix well. Sprinkle the mixture over one half of each tortilla, then fold the other half over to form a little parcel, pressing the edges together to seal. Brush the grill plate again with oil and cook the quesadillas for about 1 minute on each side, or until grill marks appear. Drain on crumpled paper towels and slice in half.

Put a grilled chicken breast on each serving plate with 2 quesadilla halves. Top the chicken with a good dollop of salsa and serve at once.

peppered tuna steaks with wasabi dressing

serves 4

4 x 250 g (9 oz) fresh **tuna steaks**

3 tablespoons **soy sauce**

3 tablespoons **cracked black pepper**

350 g (12 oz/2 bunches) **young asparagus**, trimmed and blanched

2 **red onions**, quartered

2 tablespoons **olive oil**

wasabi dressing

50 g (13/4 oz) **thick plain yoghurt**

3 tablespoons **whole-egg mayonnaise**

1 tablespoon **lemon juice**

2 teaspoons **wasabi paste**

1 tablespoon finely chopped **dill**

Preheat a barbecue grill plate, flat plate or chargrill pan to high. Toss the tuna steaks in the soy sauce, then coat liberally with the black pepper, pressing in well. Cover and refrigerate until ready to cook.

In a small bowl, combine the wasabi dressing ingredients and mix together well. Set aside until needed.

Toss the asparagus and onion in a bowl with the oil until coated all over. Grill them on the hotplate for about 5 minutes, or until the onion starts to brown. Remove from the heat and keep warm.

Put the tuna on the hotplate and cook for 3–5 minutes, turning once, or until the outside is browned and crisp — the tuna should still be a little pink in the middle. The exact cooking time will vary depending on the thickness of your tuna steaks. Slice the tuna into thick strips.

Arrange the asparagus and onion on four serving plates, top with the tuna slices and drizzle with a little wasabi dressing. Serve any remaining dressing on the side.

jumbo spicy lamb burgers

serves 4

2 **red capsicums (peppers)**

1 **eggplant (aubergine)**, cut into
  8 thick slices

3 tablespoons **olive oil**

3 teaspoons **ground cumin**

2 teaspoons **ground coriander**

1 teaspoon **ground cardamom**

1/2 teaspoon **ground cinnamon**

3 tablespoons chopped **coriander
  (cilantro) stems** and **leaves**

750 g (1 lb 10 oz) **minced (ground) lamb**

1 small **red onion**, diced

oil, for brushing

8 thick slices **sourdough bread**

200 g (7 oz) ready-made **baba ghanoush**

60 g (2 oz) **baby rocket (arugula)
  leaves**

125 g (41/2 oz/1/2 cup) **whole-egg
  mayonnaise**

3 **garlic cloves**, crushed

Heat the grill (broiler) to high. Cut the capsicums into quarters, discarding the seeds and membrane. Arrange skin-side-up on the grill tray and grill until the skin blackens and blisters. Leave to cool in a plastic bag, then peel away the skin.

Meanwhile, preheat a barbecue flat plate, grill plate or chargrill pan to high. Toss the eggplant in the oil to coat and cook for 2–3 minutes on each side, or until golden and softened. Remove from the heat. Turn the barbecue down to moderately high.

Dry-fry the ground cumin, coriander, cardamom and cinnamon in a frying pan over medium heat for 1 minute or until fragrant, taking care not to let the spices burn. Put the fried spices in a bowl with the chopped coriander, lamb and onion and season with salt and pepper. Mix until well combined, then form into four burgers about 1 cm (1/2 inch) thick.

Brush the hotplate with oil and cook the lamb burgers for 4–5 minutes on each side, or until cooked through.

Meanwhile, grill the bread until toasted on both sides. Spread the baba ghanoush over 4 of the slices and top with the rocket, eggplant, capsicum and lamb burgers. Mix the mayonnaise and garlic together and dollop over the burgers. Top with the remaining bread halves and serve immediately.

pork and polenta stack

serves 4

1.125 litres (39 fl oz/4¹/2 cups) **chicken stock**

2 teaspoons **balsamic vinegar**

1 teaspoon **Worcestershire sauce**

1 teaspoon **cornflour (cornstarch)**

150 g (5¹/2 oz/1 cup) **instant polenta**

2 tablespoons grated **parmesan cheese**

oil, for brushing

2 x 200 g (7 oz) **pork fillets**

chopped **flat-leaf (Italian) parsley**, to serve

In a small saucepan, combine 185 ml (6 fl oz/3/4 cup) of the stock with the vinegar, Worcestershire sauce and cornflour. Stir over medium heat until the mixture boils and thickens, then set aside.

In another saucepan, bring the remaining stock to the boil. Add the polenta and stir constantly over medium heat for 7 minutes, or until the mixture has thickened and the polenta is soft. Stir in the parmesan, and some salt and cracked black pepper to taste. Pour into a lightly oiled 23 cm (9 inch) square cake tin and allow to cool. Refrigerate for about 1 hour, or until firm.

Preheat a barbecue grill plate or flat plate to medium. Turn the polenta out of the tin and cut it into four squares. Lightly brush both sides with oil and cook for about 3–4 minutes on each side, or until golden all over. Set aside and keep warm.

Cut each pork fillet in half crossways. Place between two sheets of plastic wrap and rest cut-side-down on a chopping board, then gently flatten them slightly with a rolling pin or mallet. Brush the hotplate with a little more oil and cook the pork for 4 minutes on each side, or until just cooked through. Meanwhile, reheat the sauce.

Divide the polenta among four serving plates and top with a slice of pork. Drizzle with the warm sauce, sprinkle with parsley and serve with mixed vegetables.

shish kebabs with risoni salad

serves 4

risoni salad

200 g (7 oz/1 cup) **risoni**

2 teaspoons **extra virgin olive oil**

2 teaspoons **balsamic vinegar**

1/2 teaspoon grated **lemon zest**

2 teaspoons **lemon juice**

40 g (13/4 oz) **baby rocket (arugula) leaves**

11/2 tablespoons shredded **basil leaves**

1/2 small **red onion**, finely sliced

shish kebabs

250 g (9 oz) **minced (ground) lamb**

250 g (9 oz) **minced (ground) veal**

1 **onion**, finely chopped

2 **garlic cloves**, crushed

1 teaspoon **ground allspice**

1 teaspoon **ground cinnamon**

oil, for brushing

First, make the risoni salad. Bring a saucepan of salted water to the boil, add the risoni and cook for about 12 minutes, or until tender. Drain, rinse under cold water, then drain again. Put the risoni in a large bowl with the oil, vinegar, lemon zest, lemon juice, rocket, basil and onion. Mix well, season to taste with salt and pepper and refrigerate until ready to serve.

To make the shish kebabs, put the lamb, veal, onion, garlic, allspice and cinnamon in a food processor with a little salt and pepper. Blend until fine, but not mushy. Divide the mixture into eight equal portions, then roll into long sausage-shaped shish kebabs. Insert a long metal skewer through the middle of each shish kebab, pressing the mixture firmly onto the skewers. Refrigerate for 30 minutes to firm.

Preheat a barbecue grill plate, flat plate or chargrill pan to medium. Brush the hotplate with oil and grill the kebabs for about 8–10 minutes, or until cooked through, turning often. Serve warm with the risoni salad.

fresh ricotta with capsicum and chilli salad

serves 6 as a side dish

oil, for brushing

2 **yellow capsicums (peppers)**

2 **red capsicums (peppers)**

1 long **red chilli**

6 unpeeled **garlic cloves**

2 tablespoons **extra virgin olive oil**

2 teaspoons **red wine vinegar**

1/4 teaspoon **caster (superfine) sugar**

3 small handfuls **basil leaves**, roughly chopped

500 g (1 lb 2 oz) wedge fresh **ricotta cheese**

Preheat a barbecue grill plate to high. Lightly brush with oil and cook the whole capsicums for about 25 minutes, or until charred on all sides and tender. For the last 10 minutes of cooking, add the chilli and whole garlic cloves and cook until charred on all sides and tender. Put the capsicums, chilli and garlic cloves in a plastic bag and leave for about 10 minutes, or until cool enough to handle.

Peel the skin from the capsicums and chilli and slice the flesh into long thin strips, discarding the seeds and membranes. Squeeze the garlic cloves out of their skins, then chop them and toss in a bowl with the oil, vinegar and sugar. Mix well, season to taste, then mix through the capsicum, chilli and shredded basil leaves.

Cut the ricotta into six equal wedges, draining off any excess liquid if necessary. Put the ricotta wedges on their sides on six serving plates and top with the capsicum salad and some cracked black pepper. Serve warm, or at room temperature.

tip If the ricotta falls apart, press it into a mould to regain its shape.

eggplant, tahini and mint salad

serves 4 as a side dish

tahini dressing

3 tablespoons **tahini**

2 teaspoons **olive oil**

1 **garlic clove**, crushed

2 tablespoons **lemon juice**

1 large **eggplant (aubergine)**, thinly sliced

2 tablespoons **olive oil**

1 **garlic clove**, crushed

1 large handful **mint leaves**, roughly chopped

3 tablespoons chopped **parsley**

2 tablespoons **thick plain yoghurt**

1/4 teaspoon **mild smoky paprika**

Put all the tahini dressing ingredients in a food processor with 125 ml (4 fl oz/1/2 cup) of warm water. Blend until well combined and set aside until needed.

Preheat a barbecue grill plate, flat plate or chargrill pan to medium. Put the eggplant slices in a large bowl, add the oil and garlic, then toss well to coat. Cook the eggplant for about 3 minutes, or until grill marks appear, turning once. Place in a large bowl and allow to cool.

Toss the mint, parsley and tahini dressing through the eggplant slices, mixing well. Serve at room temperature, dolloped with yoghurt and sprinkled with the paprika.

pumpkin with saffron and coriander butter

serves 6 as a side dish

saffron and coriander butter

small pinch of **saffron threads**

50 g (13/4 oz) **butter**, softened

1 tablespoon finely chopped **coriander (cilantro) leaves**

1/2 **jap (kent) pumpkin**

olive oil, for brushing

3 tablespoons **coriander (cilantro) leaves**

To make the saffron and coriander butter, put the saffron in a small bowl, add 2 teaspoons of hot water and leave to soak for at least 20 minutes. Add the butter and coriander and mix until thoroughly combined. Put the butter mixture into the centre of a piece of plastic wrap, then roll up into a 7 cm (23/4 inch) log. Refrigerate for about 30 minutes, or until firm.

Preheat a barbecue grill plate or chargrill pan to high. Slice the unpeeled pumpkin into 2 cm (3/4 inch) thick wedges and discard the seeds. Brush the wedges on both sides with oil and season with salt and pepper.

Grill the pumpkin for 10 minutes on each side, or until browned and tender. Place on a serving platter and top with the sliced saffron and coriander butter. Allow the butter to melt a little and serve the pumpkin hot, scattered with coriander leaves.

polenta with corn, tomato and avocado salsa

serves 4 as a side dish

225 g (8 oz/1 1/2 cups) **instant polenta**

40 g (1 1/2 oz) **butter**, chopped

2 **garlic cloves**, crushed

olive oil, for brushing

corn, tomato and avocado salsa

2 small **corn cobs**, husks and silks
   removed

2 **tomatoes**, diced

1 small **avocado**, diced

1 teaspoon **lime juice**

1 tablespoon **olive oil**

First, prepare the polenta. Bring 1 litre (35 fl oz/4 cups) of water to the boil in a saucepan. Add 2 teaspoons of salt and gradually add the polenta in a steady stream, stirring constantly. Reduce the heat to low and cook, stirring often, until all the liquid is absorbed and the mixture comes away from the sides of the pan. This will take about 3–4 minutes. Stir in the butter and garlic and immediately pour into a lightly oiled, shallow 22 cm (8 1/2 inch) square cake tin. Level the surface with the back of a wet spoon, and leave to cool at room temperature for 20–30 minutes.

Preheat a barbecue grill plate to medium. Lightly brush with oil and cook the corn cobs, turning often, for about 8–10 minutes, or until tender and lightly browned. Take them off the heat and when they're cool enough to handle, slice the kernels off the cobs and put them in a bowl. Add the remaining salsa ingredients, season with salt and plenty of freshly ground black pepper, then toss together lightly.

Turn the cooled polenta out onto a flat surface and cut it into four squares. Cut each in half to give eight rectangles. Brush both sides well with some olive oil and barbecue for 3 minutes, or until grill lines appear. Turn and cook the other side for another 3 minutes, or until grill lines appear. Divide the polenta between four serving plates and top with a spoonful of salsa. Serve hot.

skewered garlic and cumin mushrooms

serves 4 as a side dish

16 **button mushrooms**
4 tablespoons **olive oil**
1 **garlic clove**, crushed
1/2 teaspoon **ground cumin**
2 tablespoons chopped **parsley**
1 **lemon**, cut into 4 wedges

Soak four bamboo skewers in cold water for 30 minutes. Preheat a barbecue grill plate, flat plate or chargrill pan to medium.

Trim the ends of the mushroom stalks, but don't cut them off completely. Put the oil, garlic, cumin and some salt and cracked black pepper in a bowl. Add the mushrooms and toss to coat.

Thread 4 mushrooms onto each skewer, piercing them through the stalk. Barbecue the mushrooms, turning occasionally and brushing with any remaining oil mixture, for about 5 minutes, or until soft and lightly browned. Place on a serving plate, sprinkle with parsley, add a squeeze of lemon and serve.

potato rösti with bacon and sage

makes 12

20 g (3/4 oz) **butter**

1 **onion**, grated

1 **garlic clove**, crushed

2 slices **bacon**, finely chopped

600 g (1 lb 5 oz) **all-purpose potatoes**, such as desiree, peeled and
coarsely grated

1–2 tablespoons finely chopped **sage leaves**

olive oil, for brushing

Melt the butter in a large frying pan. Add the onion, garlic and bacon and cook over medium heat, stirring, for about 5 minutes, or until soft. Add the grated potato and cook, stirring, for 1–2 minutes, or until the mixture is sticky. Remove from the heat and stir in the sage and some salt and cracked black pepper. Mix well, then spread onto a flat tray and leave until cool enough to handle.

Preheat a barbecue flat plate or grill plate to moderately high. Divide the potato mixture into 12 portions and shape each portion into evenly sized patties.

Brush the hotplate generously with oil. Cook the rösti in batches for 3–5 minutes on each side, or until golden brown and crisp, pressing each rösti to a 5 cm (2 inch) round using a spatula, taking care not to loosen the mixture. Drain on crumpled paper towels and serve hot.

chargrilled haloumi with orange and walnut salad

serves 4 as a side dish

4 **oranges**

400 g (14 oz) **haloumi cheese**

3 tablespoons **olive oil**

1 large handful **flat-leaf (Italian) parsley leaves**, torn

3 tablespoons **mint leaves**, torn

2 teaspoons **red wine vinegar**

70 g (21/2 oz/3/4 cup) **walnuts**, toasted and roughly chopped

1/2 teaspoon **sumac** (see tip)

Cut the base and top off each orange, then cut away the skin in a downward motion just deep enough to remove all the white membrane. Cut each orange into 1 cm (1/2 inch) thick slices. Arrange them over the base of a large flat serving dish, overlapping the slices slightly, and set aside.

Preheat a barbecue grill plate, flat plate or chargrill pan to medium. Pat the haloumi dry with paper towels and cut into 1 cm (1/2 inch) thick batons. Brush the hotplate with a little of the oil and cook the haloumi for 5–6 minutes, or until golden on all sides. Drain on crumpled paper towels, then arrange the haloumi over the oranges and scatter with the parsley and mint.

If you are cooking on a barbecue plate, put the vinegar in a small saucepan and place it on the hotplate; if you are using a chargrill pan, heat the vinegar and other ingredients in the chargrill pan instead. Swirl the vinegar around for 30 seconds, then add the walnuts and cook for another minute, tossing constantly. Pour immediately over the salad mixture. Sprinkle with the sumac and a little freshly ground black pepper and serve at once.

tip Sumac is a spice widely used in Lebanese and Turkish cuisine. It is a dried, crushed berry with an astringent lemon flavour.

grilled tomato turkish bread

serves 4–6 as a side dish

1 large **Turkish bread**

140 g (5 oz/1/2 cup) **sun-dried tomato pesto**

1 tablespoon **olive oil**

1 tablespoon finely chopped **rosemary leaves**

1 tablespoon **tomato paste (purée)**

1/2 teaspoon **caster (superfine) sugar**

1 **garlic clove**, crushed

150 g (51/2 oz/1 cup) grated **mozzarella cheese**

Preheat a barbecue flat plate to low. Meanwhile, split the Turkish bread in half along the middle.

Combine the tomato pesto, oil, rosemary, tomato paste, sugar and garlic in a small bowl and mix well. Spread the mixture over both cut sides of the bread, then sprinkle one side with the cheese and sandwich together with the other half.

Wrap the bread firmly in a double layer of foil and cook on the hotplate for about 3 minutes on each side, or until the bread is crisp and the cheese has melted. Serve immediately.

corn with chilli lime butter

serves 6 as a side dish

6 **corn cobs**, husks and silks removed

75 g (2¹/2 oz) **butter**, at room temperature

1 tablespoon finely chopped **coriander (cilantro) leaves**

1 small **red chilli**, finely chopped

2 teaspoons **lime juice**

6 **lime wedges**

Preheat a barbecue grill plate or chargrill pan to moderately hot. Lightly brush the hotplate with oil and grill the cobs for about 15 minutes, turning often, until tender and flecked with brown.

Meanwhile, put the butter in a small bowl and mash with a fork. Add the coriander, chilli and lime juice and mix together until well combined.

When the cobs are cooked, secure corn holders in each end and spread each cob with some chilli lime butter. Season with salt and serve each cob with a wedge of lime for squeezing over the top.

covered grill

going undercover

Covered grills impart a flavour to cooked foods all their own: smoky, succulent and searingly seductive. They are essentially an outdoor oven, and their distinguishing feature is that they have a lid that can be lowered, enabling you to roast, grill or smoke food. There are two types of covered grill: a covered barbecue, which has a fitted lid or hood that you can pull down over the food for roasting or slow-cooking; and a kettle-style barbecue, which is a round barbecue with a large domed lid. If you don't have a covered grill, don't despair: you can create the same effect on a conventional barbecue by inverting a large metal bowl or wok over the food, or by covering smaller quantities of food with a large tent of foil. The basic cooking principle is still the same.

how it works

Covered grills are excellent for indirect cooking, where larger chunks of meat or poultry are cooked with the heat source positioned on the sides and not directly underneath the food. The cooking time is longer than in a conventional oven, but the meat is moister and much more succulent, with a distinctive barbecue flavour. These type of grills also control heat efficiently — the more heat retained, the less fuel used.

Kettle-style barbecues generally have a rounded base which contains a rack holding the heat source, then a metal grill over the top. Opening and closing the air vents helps regulate the temperature. The more open the vents, the hotter the fuel will burn. Closing the vents reduces the airflow and consequently the cooking temperature.

for best results

When cooking large cuts of meat such as a leg of lamb in a covered grill, first quickly sear it on all sides on the hottest part of the grill to seal in all the juices — there's no need to have the lid down at this stage. The meat can then be cooked directly on the grill over indirect heat, or placed in a roasting tin or foil container on the grill before lowering the cover (the individual recipe will tell you what to do). You usually won't need to turn the meat, as it will cook through on all sides, much as it would in a convection oven. If the meat is being cooked in a roasting tin or foil container, the pan juices can be poured over the top or used as a baste to ensure the meat stays moist, or they can be used to make a sauce. Avoid lifting the lid too often during cooking as this will let heat escape, resulting in a longer cooking time. This is especially important when smoking foods.

dry smoking

Soak your woodchips in **cold water** for at least 30 minutes before use, or even overnight.

If using **charcoal**, make sure it is **fully heated**, then arrange the soaked woodchips over the **top**.

Put the grill **rack** over the heat source, then sit the food on a **foil parcel** over the woodchips.

Carefully **lift up** the lid when the cooking time has **expired** to check if the food is ready.

smoking food

Smoking is a simple process yielding superb results. Special woodchips (sold in barbecue and outdoor stores in many different varieties) give off a wonderfully scented smoke and infuse food with their aroma. However, it is important to never use wood that is not specifically intended for smoking food, as many varieties of wood are chemically treated and may make the food poisonous. In particular, pine, cedar and eucalyptus produce acrid smoke and are unsuitable for cooking.

Woodchips must be soaked for at least 30 minutes before use (follow the packet instructions). To smoke food in a gas grill, put the soaked woodchips in a smokebox (a heavy, cast-iron receptacle with a removable lid), or make your own simple smokebox by folding several layers of foil into a boat shape and punching several holes in it (disposable foil trays are also good). Set the smokebox on top of the briquettes, or on the rack over the heat source to the side of the grill. The food is then placed on the rack above the heat source, in the path of the rising smoke, to allow the smoke to penetrate during cooking. Herbs and spices can also be added to the smokebox, and for a more intense smoked flavour, you can use more than one container.

When using a charcoal grill, spread the woodchips directly on the coals. To smoke food in a kettle barbecue, prepare it for indirect cooking, following the manufacturer's instructions; add the woodchips and close the lid until the woodchips begin to smoke, then add the food. Lift the lid as little as possible during cooking to keep the smoke in.

The method of smoking described above is referred to as dry smoking, but you could also try wet smoking, in which a pan of water is placed between the food and coals to put humidity into the cooking environment. Beer or wine can be added to the water for extra flavour. This method takes slightly longer than dry smoking.

guide to cooking times

The cooking temperature in a covered grill can vary quite a bit so here is an approximate guide to cooking different meats.

Beef requires different cooking times depending on whether your cut of meat contains a bone. For every 500 g (1 lb 2 oz) of beef with a bone, allow 15 minutes for rare, 20 minutes for medium and 25 minutes for meat well done. For the same amount of beef without a bone, allow 10 minutes for rare, 15 minutes for medium and 20 minutes for well done.

When cooking a leg of lamb, for every 500 g (1 lb 2 oz) allow 10–15 minutes for medium rare, 20–25 minutes for medium and 30 minutes for well done.

For pork, allow 30 minutes of cooking time for every 500 g (1 lb 2 oz). It is important to avoid overcooking pork as the flesh will become dry. To test if it is properly cooked, insert a skewer into the thickest portion or near the bone: the juices should run clear, with no hint of pink.

Whole poultry requires 20–25 minutes per 500 g (1 lb 2 oz). Chicken must be cooked right through, with no pink flesh near the bone. To check if it's done, insert a skewer between the thigh and body right through to the bone: the juices should run clear.

Different species of fish need different cooking times; however, as a rule of thumb, allow 20–25 minutes per 500 g (1 lb 2 oz). Some fish, such as salmon and tuna steaks, are often served medium rare so the flesh doesn't dry out — depending on their thickness, they may only need a few minutes on each side over direct heat. Most other types of fish are generally cooked through. Whatever type of fish or seafood you are cooking, remove it from the heat as soon as it is ready as the residual heat in the fish will keep cooking the delicate flesh. To test whether fish is ready, insert a thin-bladed knife into the thickest portion: the flesh should flake cleanly.

beef fillet with caramelized onion and horseradish cream

serves 4

2 tablespoons **olive oil**

2 **garlic cloves**, crushed

5 **thyme sprigs**, plus extra, to serve

1.25 kg (2 lb 12 oz) piece **beef fillet**

caramelized onion

1 1/2 tablespoons **olive oil**

3 **red onions**, thinly sliced

1 tablespoon **soft brown sugar**

horseradish cream

125 ml (4 fl oz/1/2 cup) **thick (double/heavy) cream**

75 g (2 3/4 oz/1/4 cup) ready-made **horseradish sauce**

1 **garlic clove**, crushed

1 tablespoon **lemon juice**

Mix together the oil, garlic and thyme, and season with salt and freshly ground black pepper. Brush the mixture all over the beef, ensuring it is thoroughly coated.

Preheat a kettle or covered barbecue to medium indirect heat. Put the beef in a baking dish and place it on the rack in the middle of the barbecue. Lower the lid and cook for 40 minutes for medium rare. Remove the beef from the heat, cover loosely with foil and leave to rest until ready to serve.

While the beef is cooking, caramelize the onions. Heat the oil in a saucepan over medium heat. Add the onions and cook for 2–3 minutes, or until slightly softened. Turn the heat down to low and cook the onions for another 15 minutes, stirring occasionally, until they start to caramelize. Stir in the sugar and cook for a further 5 minutes, or until caramelized.

Put the horseradish cream ingredients in a small bowl. Mix well, season to taste with freshly ground black pepper and refrigerate until needed.

Once the beef has rested, cut it into 1 cm (1/2 inch) thick slices. Arrange the beef on four serving plates and top with the horseradish cream and caramelized onion. Scatter with some thyme sprigs and serve at once, with steamed potatoes.

Brush the oil, garlic and thyme **all over** the beef, making sure it is well coated.

Gently cook the onions over **low heat**, stirring now and then, until caramelized.

287

barbecued pizza with mozzarella, prosciutto and basil

serves 4

pizza base

11/4 teaspoons **dried yeast**

1/4 teaspoon **salt**

1/4 teaspoon **caster (superfine) sugar**

155 g (51/2 oz/11/4 cups) **plain (all-purpose) flour**

topping

125 g (41/2 oz/1/2 cup) **herb and garlic tomato passata (puréed tomatoes)**

8 slices **prosciutto**

125 g (41/2 oz) **mozzarella cheese,** sliced into thin rounds

12 **basil leaves**

1 tablespoon **extra virgin olive oil**

Put the yeast, salt and sugar in a bowl. Quickly stir in 170 ml (51/2 fl oz/2/3 cup) of tepid water, then cover and leave in a warm place for 10–15 minutes, or until the mixture is foamy. If the mixture doesn't foam, the yeast is dead and you will need to start again.

Put the flour in a bowl and make a well in the centre. Pour in the yeast mixture and bring together with a wooden spoon to form a soft dough. Put in an oiled bowl, then cover and leave in a warm place for about 30 minutes, or until doubled in size.

While the dough is rising, preheat a kettle or covered barbecue to medium indirect heat. Turn the pizza dough out onto a lightly floured surface and knead gently. Using the palms of your hands or a rolling pin, press or roll the dough out into a thin circle about 35 cm (14 inches) in diameter. Put the pizza base in a lightly oiled, shallow-sided 30 cm (12 inch) non-stick frying pan with a metal handle, then roll over the edges to form a 1 cm (1/2 inch) rim.

Spread the passata evenly over the pizza base. Arrange the prosciutto on top and scatter with the mozzarella. Sit the pan on a cake rack on the barbecue plate, then lower the lid and cook for 12 minutes, or until the pizza base is golden and crispy. Wearing gloves or oven mitts, take the pan off the heat (the handle will be very hot). Scatter with the basil, drizzle with the oil, then cut into wedges and serve.

smoked trout and kipfler potato salad

serves 4

6 **hickory woodchips**

2 **rainbow trout**

1 tablespoon **oil**

750 g (1 lb 10 oz) even-sized **kipfler (fingerling) potatoes**, peeled

3 **baby fennel bulbs**, cut into quarters, then into eighths

2 tablespoons **olive oil**

40 g (1 1/2 oz/2 cups) **watercress sprigs**

dill and caper dressing

125 g (4 1/2 oz/1/2 cup) **whole-egg mayonnaise**

2 **garlic cloves**, crushed

1 tablespoon chopped **dill**

1 tablespoon **baby capers**, drained, rinsed and chopped

1 tablespoon **lemon juice**

Soak the woodchips in water overnight, or for a minimum of 30 minutes.

Preheat a kettle or covered barbecue to low indirect heat. Allow the coals to burn down to ash, then add three hickory woodchips to each pile of coals. When the chips begin to smoke, brush the trout with the oil, place in the middle of the barbecue, then lower the lid and cook for 10–15 minutes, or until the trout are cooked through. (If you don't have a coal barbecue, use the method outlined on page 322 for smoking racks of lamb.)

Meanwhile, preheat the barbecue chargrill plate to medium–high and bring a saucepan of water to the boil on the stovetop. Add the potatoes to the pan and cook for 5 minutes, or until almost tender. Drain well and allow to cool slightly. Combine the dill and caper dressing ingredients in a small bowl and refrigerate until needed.

Cut the potatoes into 1.5 cm (5/8 inch) slices on the diagonal. Place in a bowl with the fennel and olive oil, season with salt and freshly ground black pepper and toss to coat. Chargrill the potatoes for 5 minutes on each side, or until golden and cooked. Remove from the heat and place in a serving bowl. Chargrill the fennel for 2–3 minutes on each side, or until golden, then add to the potato slices.

Remove the skin from the smoked trout and gently pull the flesh away from the bones. Flake the flesh into pieces and add to the potato with the watercress and fennel. Pour on the dressing and serve immediately.

spatchcock with mandarin butter

serves 4

4 **spatchcocks (poussin)**

125 g (4¹/₂ oz) **butter**, softened

2 **garlic cloves**, crushed

1 teaspoon **mandarin oil** (see tip)

¹/₂ teaspoon tinned **green peppercorns**, drained and finely chopped

Preheat a kettle or covered barbecue to indirect medium–low heat. Cut each spatchcock down each side of the backbone using a large knife or kitchen shears. Discard the backbones, then remove and discard the necks. Turn the spatchcocks over and press down on the breastbone to flatten them out. Remove and discard any excess fat, skin and innards, then rinse well and pat dry with paper towels.

In a small bowl, mix together the butter, garlic, mandarin oil and peppercorns. Push two fingers under the skin of the spatchcock breasts on either side of the central membrane to form two pockets (it doesn't matter if the membrane comes away as well). Gently push a heaped teaspoon of the butter mixture into each pocket, then rub the remaining butter mixture all over each bird.

Sit a rectangular cake rack on the barbecue plate and rest the spatchcocks on top, skin-side-up. Lower the lid and roast for about 40–45 minutes, or until the birds are golden brown and the juices run clear when tested with a skewer in the thickest part of the thigh. Alternatively, test the birds using a meat thermometer — they will be cooked when the temperature reaches 85°C (185°F). Serve with baked potato wedges and lightly steamed vegetables.

tip If you can't get mandarin oil, use orange oil instead, which you can make by infusing 1 tablespoon olive oil with 2 teaspoons of grated orange zest.

Cut along both sides of the spatchcock backbone and **discard** it.

Make a **pocket** in the skin over each spatchcock breast and **fill with** the herbed butter.

pork with bacon and baby apples

serves 6

1.5 kg (3 lb 5 oz) **rolled pork loin roast**

6 slices **bacon**

600 ml (21 fl oz) **apple juice**

12 **baby red apples** or 3 **small ripe red apples**, halved but not cored

Preheat a kettle or covered barbecue to medium indirect heat. Remove the string from around the pork loin, then the skin. Sprinkle the pork generously with freshly ground black pepper and wrap the bacon slices around the loin to cover it completely. Sit the pork on a rack in a large roasting tin and pour on 375 ml (13 fl oz/1½ cups) of the apple juice.

Place the roasting tin on the barbecue grill, lower the lid and cook the pork for 15–20 minutes, checking now and then that the apple juice isn't evaporating too quickly from the roasting tin — if it is, top it up with extra apple juice.

Reduce the heat to low, baste the pork with the roasting juices and cook for another 20 minutes, basting and adding more apple juice as needed.

Add the apples to the pork and coat them with the roasting tin juices. Baste the pork again, add more apple juice to the roasting tin if needed, and cook for another 40 minutes, or until the juices run clear when tested with a skewer in the thickest part. Alternatively, test the pork using a meat thermometer — it will be cooked when the temperature reaches 75°C (167°F). During roasting, baste the pork regularly with the roasting juices and top up with apple juice as needed.

Take the pork off the heat, transfer to a plate with the apples and cover loosely with foil, then leave to rest for 10 minutes. Meanwhile, check the pan juices — if they look a little thin, pour them into a small pan and simmer over low heat, stirring with a wooden spoon, until they reach the desired consistency. Season to taste. Serve the pork with the apples and pan juices, perhaps with some sautéed red cabbage and boiled baby potatoes.

chicken marylands with currants and pine nut stuffing

serves 4

pine nut stuffing

80 g (2¾ oz/1 cup) **fresh breadcrumbs**

20 g (¾ oz) **butter**, melted

2 tablespoons **lemon juice**

1 teaspoon grated **lemon zest**

35 g (1¼ oz/¼ cup) **currants**

40 g (1½ oz/¼ cup) **pine nuts**

2 teaspoons **thyme leaves**

4 x 375 g (13 oz) **chicken Marylands (leg quarters)**, with skin on

1 **garlic clove**, halved

1/2 **lemon**

375 ml (13 fl oz/1½ cups) **chicken stock**

Preheat a kettle or covered barbecue to medium indirect heat. Meanwhile, put all the pine nut stuffing ingredients in a bowl and mix together well.

Rub each chicken portion with the cut side of the garlic clove and the lemon. Using your fingers, gently push the stuffing under the skin of each chicken portion, then secure with a small skewer or thick toothpick.

Put the chicken in a roasting tin, pour on the stock, then put the tin on the barbecue grill and lower the lid. Roast for 30 minutes, or until the juices run clear when tested with a skewer in the thickest part of the thigh. During cooking, baste the chicken regularly and top up the stock a little at a time as it evaporates to ensure the chicken stays moist. Serve the chicken hot, with roast vegetables and steamed green beans, if desired.

whole ocean trout in banana leaves

serves 8

2.5 kg (5 lb 8 oz) whole cleaned **ocean trout**

150 g (51/2 oz/3/4 cup) roughly chopped fresh **ginger**

3 stems **lemon grass**, white part only, sliced

18 **makrut (kaffir lime) leaves**

125 ml (4 fl oz/1/2 cup) **vegetable oil**

2 teaspoons **sea salt**

2 **lemons**, sliced

2 large **banana leaves**, halved lengthways, centre vein removed

lemon or **lime wedges**, to serve

Wash the trout in cold water, then pat dry inside and out with paper towels. Cut five deep slashes on each side of the trout.

Put the ginger, lemon grass and 12 of the lime leaves in a food processor with the oil and salt. Blend to a paste. Rub the paste inside the cavity of the fish and all over the skin, rubbing well into the slits. Put the lemon slices and remaining lime leaves in the cavity of the trout, then sit the fish in a large dish, cover and refrigerate for several hours to allow the flavours to develop.

Meanwhile, preheat a kettle or covered barbecue to medium indirect heat.

Bring a large saucepan of water to the boil. If the banana leaves are too large for the pan, cut them in half. Add the banana leaves in batches and simmer for 2 minutes, or until softened slightly. Remove and refresh in cold water.

Put the banana leaves on a work surface, overlapping them slightly. Now place the trout in the centre of the leaves, and carefully enclose the trout so it is fully covered by banana leaves. Tie into a parcel at frequent intervals with kitchen string.

Rest the trout on a cake rack and sit it on the barbecue grill. Lower the lid and cook for about 30 minutes, then carefully turn the trout over using two large spatulas (you may need someone to help you do this). Grill for another 30 minutes, or until the trout is just cooked through.

To serve, put the trout on a large platter, then carefully cut and remove the string. Cut along the centre of the banana leaves and open them up to expose the trout. Gently peel back the skin of the trout and carefully lift out large pieces of fish. Serve with fresh lemon or lime wedges, and a green salad and crusty bread, if desired.

tip Banana leaves are often available at speciality fruit and vegetable stores.

Cut five deep slits **along each side** of the trout to let the flavours penetrate.

Rub the paste all over the fish, and put the **lemon** slices and lime leaves inside it.

peppered beef on udon noodles

serves 4

3 teaspoons **cracked black pepper**

3 teaspoons **shichimi togarashi seasoning** (see tip)

4 x 150 g (5½ oz) **beef fillets**

400 g (14 oz) **udon noodles**

oil, for brushing

2 **baby fennel bulbs**, trimmed and quartered

1 tablespoon **vegetable oil**

2 tablespoons **light soy sauce**

2 **spring onions (scallions)**, finely sliced on the diagonal

Preheat a kettle or covered barbecue chargrill to low–medium indirect heat.

Put the pepper and shichimi togarashi seasoning in a small bowl and mix well. Spread the mixture over both sides of the beef fillets, pressing in well. Cover with plastic wrap and refrigerate until ready to use.

Put the noodles in a heatproof bowl, cover with boiling water and leave for 3 minutes. (Alternatively, cook the noodles according to the packet instructions.) Rinse the noodles and drain well.

Brush the grill plate lightly with oil. Add the beef and fennel, then lower the lid and cook for 4 minutes. Turn the beef and fennel and cook for a further 3 minutes (the steaks will be medium to well done). Remove the steaks, cover loosely with foil and allow to rest for 5–10 minutes. Barbecue the fennel for several more minutes, or until soft and cooked. Slice the beef into thin strips and keep warm.

Heat a wok over medium–high heat, add the vegetable oil and swirl to coat. Add the noodles and stir-fry for 2 minutes, or until heated through. Arrange a nest of noodles on four serving plates. Top with the fennel, then the beef fillets. Drizzle with the soy sauce, sprinkle with the spring onion and serve.

tip Shichimi togarashi, also known as Japanese seven-spice, is a peppery seasoning available from Japanese and speciality food stores.

spicy leg of lamb with herbed crust

serves 6–8

marinade

125 ml (4 fl oz/1/2 cup) **olive oil**

125 ml (4 fl oz/1/2 cup) **white wine**

3 tablespoons **lemon juice**

2 **garlic cloves**, crushed

1 teaspoon **ground coriander**

1 teaspoon **ground cumin**

1 teaspoon **freshly ground
   black pepper**

1 kg (2 lb 4 oz) **leg of lamb**, boned

oil, for brushing

herbed crust

21/2 large handfuls **basil leaves**

4 large handfuls **coriander
   (cilantro) leaves**

2 tablespoons **pine nuts**

2 **garlic cloves**, crushed

3 tablespoons **olive oil**

25 g (1 oz/1/4 cup) finely grated
   parmesan cheese

40 g (11/2 oz/1/2 cup) **fresh white
   breadcrumbs**

Put all the marinade ingredients in a non-metallic bowl and mix together well. Cut a series of small diagonal slits into the lamb, then put the lamb in a shallow non-metallic dish and pour the marinade over. Cover and refrigerate for 2 hours.

Heat a kettle or covered barbecue to high. While the plate is heating, make the herbed crust. Put the basil, coriander, pine nuts and garlic in a food processor and blend until finely chopped. Add the oil and parmesan and blend until combined. Transfer to a bowl, mix the breadcrumbs through and season to taste. If the mixture is a little dry, add a little more olive oil.

Brush the barbecue hotplate lightly with oil. Remove the lamb from the marinade and cook for about 5 minutes on both sides, or until well browned and sealed. Remove from the heat and place on a double sheet of foil.

Spread the herbed crust onto the lamb and press down firmly. Seal the lamb in the foil, bringing the ends of the foil together at the top and rolling them down like a parcel. Put the lamb on the barbecue, then lower the lid and roast for 35–40 minutes for medium rare, or until cooked to your liking. Cover and rest for 10–15 minutes, then slice and serve with creamed potatoes and steamed vegetables.

rolled fish fillets with lemon dill cream

serves 4

1 **lemon**

8 x 70 g (2¹/2 oz) skinless **sole** or **flathead fillets**, bones removed

8 **dill sprigs**

lemon dill cream

125 ml (4 fl oz/¹/2 cup) **white wine**

125 ml (4 fl oz/¹/2 cup) **fish** or **chicken stock**

¹/2 small **onion**, finely chopped

250 ml (9 fl oz/1 cup) **cream (whipping)**

¹/2 teaspoon finely grated **lemon zest**

3 tablespoons **lemon juice**

30 g (1 oz) **unsalted butter**, chopped

2 tablespoons chopped **dill**

Preheat a kettle or covered barbecue to medium indirect heat.

Peel the rind and the white pith from the lemon. Using a small sharp knife, cut between the lemon membranes to release the fruit segments.

Coil each fish fillet around 1 or 2 lemon segments and a sprig of dill, leaving the dill poking up through the top. Secure with a toothpick and season with salt and freshly ground black pepper. Transfer to a lightly oiled disposable foil tray and place on the barbecue. Lower the lid and cook for 20 minutes, or until the fish flakes when tested with a fork.

While the fish is cooking, make the lemon dill cream. Put the wine, stock and onion in a small saucepan and simmer for 10–15 minutes, or until reduced to 80 ml (2 1/2 fl oz/1/3 cup). Stir in the cream, lemon zest and lemon juice and simmer for a further 2–3 minutes, or until thickened slightly. Remove from the heat, strain to remove the onion, then stir in the butter and dill. Add salt and freshly ground black pepper to taste.

Arrange 2 fish coils on each serving plate. Remove the skewers and drizzle with the lemon dill cream. Serve with steamed green beans and baby potatoes.

Peel the lemon, then **cut** between each membrane to **release** the fruit segments.

Coil the fish **around** the lemon segments and dill sprigs, then **secure** with a toothpick.

asian-flavoured roast chicken

serves 4–6

glaze

2 tablespoons **honey**

2 tablespoons **soft brown sugar**

2 tablespoons **soy sauce**

1/2 teaspoon **five-spice powder**

1 tablespoon **sherry**

1 tablespoon chopped fresh **ginger**

2 **garlic cloves**, chopped

2 teaspoons **sesame oil**

1.5 kg (3 lb 5 oz) **whole chicken**

4 **star anise**, broken

2 **cinnamon sticks**, broken

5 cm (2 inch) piece fresh **ginger**, peeled and chopped

2 **garlic cloves**, chopped

1 small **onion**, thickly sliced

Preheat a kettle or covered barbecue to medium indirect heat.

To prepare the glaze, put all the ingredients in a small saucepan and stir over low heat until the sugar has dissolved. Simmer for 2 minutes, then drain and allow to cool.

Wash the chicken well with cold water and pat dry with paper towels. Fill the cavity with the star anise, cinnamon sticks, ginger, garlic and onion. Tie the legs together with kitchen string and tuck the wings up underneath the body. Sit the chicken in a lightly oiled disposable foil tray and brush lightly with some of the glaze (reserve the remaining glaze for basting).

Put the tray on the barbecue, lower the lid and roast the chicken, brushing with the glaze occasionally during cooking, for about 1 hour, or until the juices run clear when tested with a skewer in the thickest part of the thigh. Serve with rice and steamed Asian vegetables such as baby bok choy (pak choy) or choy sum.

ballotine of turkey

serves 8

50 g (1 3/4 oz) **butter**

1 **red onion**, finely chopped

3 **garlic cloves**, crushed

10 slices **prosciutto**, finely chopped

200 g (7 oz) **button mushrooms**, chopped

2 tablespoons chopped **sage leaves**

2 teaspoons finely grated **lemon zest**

125 g (41/2 oz/11/2 cups) **fresh breadcrumbs**

4 kg (9 lb) **turkey**, fully boned (see tip)

Put the **stuffing** along the bottom edge of the flattened turkey, then **roll up** tightly.

Truss the rolled-up turkey with kitchen **string** to **secure** the stuffing.

Preheat a kettle or covered barbecue to medium indirect heat.

To make the stuffing, melt the butter in a large frying pan over medium heat. Add the onion and cook for 2–3 minutes, or until softened. Add the garlic, prosciutto, mushroom and sage and cook for 3 minutes, stirring occasionally. Transfer to a bowl and stir in the lemon zest, breadcrumbs and some salt and freshly ground black pepper to taste. Remove from the heat and allow to cool.

Put the turkey on a flat surface and open it out. Pat dry with paper towels. Pound the thicker parts with a rolling pin or mallet to flatten the turkey out to an even thickness. Spread the stuffing into a log shape near the bottom edge of the turkey, leaving a 2 cm (3/4 inch) border at either side of the log. Roll the turkey up tightly, then truss at regular intervals with kitchen string. Secure the ends with toothpicks to seal the stuffing in.

Sit the turkey on a rack in a large baking dish and put it on the barbecue. Lower the lid and cook for 11/2 hours, or until the juices run clear when tested with a skewer. Remove from the heat, cover with foil and leave to rest for 10 minutes. Cut into slices and serve with roasted vegetables or salad.

tip You will need to order your boned turkey in advance from a butcher or speciality chicken shop.

marinated beef ribs in dark ale and mustard

serves 4

4 **beef spare ribs** (total weight about 2 kg/4 lb 8 oz), halved (see tip)

125 ml (4 fl oz/1/2 cup) **dark ale beer**

2 tablespoons **soft brown sugar**

3 tablespoons **cider vinegar**

2 small **red chillies**, seeded and finely chopped

2 tablespoons **ground cumin**

1 tablespoon **seeded mustard**

20 g (3/4 oz) **unsalted butter**

Arrange the ribs in a shallow non-metallic dish. Put the ale, sugar, vinegar, chilli, cumin and mustard in a large bowl, stir well to dissolve the sugar and pour over the ribs. Toss to coat, then cover and marinate in the refrigerator for 1–2 hours.

Preheat a kettle or covered barbecue to medium indirect heat. Put the ribs in a large shallow roasting tin and place it in the middle of the barbecue. Lower the lid and cook for 50 minutes, or until the meat is tender and about 125 ml (4 fl oz/1/2 cup) of liquid is left in the roasting tin. Transfer the ribs to a serving plate.

While the barbecue is still hot, put the roasting tin with all its juices over direct heat to warm through. Using a whisk, beat in the butter and season with salt and freshly ground black pepper. Arrange the ribs on four serving plates and drizzle with the warm sauce. Serve with baked potatoes and steamed greens.

tip Ask your butcher to cut the ribs in half for you as it is very difficult to do this at home.

rosemary-smoked lamb rack with minted broad beans

serves 4

2 cups **hickory woodchips**

2 x **6-cutlet racks of lamb**

4 very long **rosemary sprigs**

1 teaspoon **smoky paprika**

1 teaspoon **salt**

1/2 teaspoon **freshly ground black pepper**

1 tablespoon **oil**

1 **red capsicum (pepper)**, quartered

500 g (1 lb 2 oz) **frozen broad beans**

40 g (11/2 oz) **butter**

1 tablespoon **olive oil**

1 **garlic clove**, finely chopped

pinch of **sugar**

2 tablespoons chopped **mint leaves**

Soak the woodchips in cold water for at least 1 hour, or overnight. Drain and place in two small, disposable foil trays. Put a tray on either side of the grill in a kettle or covered barbecue. Preheat the barbecue to medium indirect heat.

Trim the lamb cutlets of excess fat, then trim and clean the exposed bones. Cut a shallow criss-cross pattern in the fatty side of the lamb. Using a thick wooden skewer, pierce two holes through the centre of the meaty parts of each lamb rack and insert a long sprig of rosemary into each one, all the way through. Combine the paprika, salt, pepper and oil in a small bowl and brush the mixture all over the lamb.

While the barbecue grill is heating up, add the capsicum, skin-side-down, and grill until the skin blackens and blisters. Leave to cool in a plastic bag, then peel away the skin and cut the flesh into long thin strips.

When the grill is smoking, stand the lamb upright in a large roasting tin, with the bones interlocking. Put the tin in the centre of the grill plate, then lower the lid and roast for 20 minutes for medium rare, or until cooked to your liking. Remove from the heat, cover loosely with foil and allow to rest. (If using a gas barbecue, put the lamb directly over the heat.)

While the lamb is resting, put the broad beans in a large saucepan of lightly salted boiling water. Cook for 2 minutes, then drain, refresh in cold water and drain again. Remove and discard the tough outer skins.

Melt the butter and oil in a frying pan. Add the garlic and capsicum and cook over medium heat for 5 minutes, or until fragrant. Add the broad beans, sugar, and salt and freshly ground black pepper to taste. Toss gently until heated through, then stir in the mint. Serve the vegetables hot with the lamb racks placed on top, allowing 3 cutlets per person.

Score a **crisscross** pattern in the lamb's fatty skin and **brush** with the paprika oil.

Stand the racks in a large roasting tin, with the **bones interlocking**.

spicy whole snapper with a wine butter sauce

serves 4

1 kg (2 lb 4 oz) **whole snapper**, cleaned and scaled

2 **celery stalks**, sliced on the diagonal

2 **red capsicums (peppers)**, sliced on the diagonal

3 **spring onions (scallions)**, thinly sliced

125 ml (4 fl oz/1/2 cup) **white wine**

1 tablespoon **shichimi togarashi** or **nanami togarashi seasoning** (see tip)

1 **lemon**, halved lengthways and thinly sliced

40 g (11/2 oz) **unsalted butter**, chopped

Preheat a kettle or covered barbecue to medium indirect heat.

Trim the snapper fins using a pair of kitchen scissors. Wash the fish well and pat dry with paper towels. Take two sheets of foil large enough to encase the fish and lay them on a flat surface. Top with the same amount of baking paper. Fold the edges into a tight, secure seam to form a large waterproof casing for the fish.

Spread the celery, capsicum and spring onion in the centre of the baking paper, then lay the fish lengthways over the vegetables. Pour the wine over and around the fish and sprinkle generously with salt, freshly ground black pepper and the Japanese seasoning. Overlap the lemon slices along the centre of the fish, then dot with butter and enclose the paper over the fish. Fold the ends in several times to seal in the liquid.

Put the fish parcel on the barbecue grill, then lower the lid and cook for about 15 minutes, or until the fish flakes when tested in the thickest part with a fork. Serve hot, with rice and lightly steamed green vegetables.

tip Shichimi togarashi is also known as Japanese seven-spice and is often sprinkled over Japanese noodle dishes, soups and one-pots. This peppery, spicy seasoning generally contains a mixture of dried red chilli flakes, black pepper, sesame seeds, poppy seeds, hemp seeds, seaweed flakes and dried mandarin or orange peel. Nanami togarashi is a similar seasoning. They are both available from Japanese and speciality food stores.

mussels with dill and capers

serves 4 as a starter

125 ml (4 fl oz/1/2 cup) **cream (whipping)**

zest of 1 **lemon**

4 tablespoons **dill sprigs**

2 tablespoons **baby capers**, rinsed and drained

10 **pitted black olives**

1 kg (2 lb 4 oz) **black mussels**, scrubbed, beards removed

3 tablespoons **white wine**

2 **garlic cloves**, crushed

70 g (21/2 oz) **butter**, chopped

4 **spring onions (scallions)**, finely sliced

Preheat a kettle or covered barbecue to medium direct heat. Mix together the cream, lemon zest, dill, capers and olives.

Put the mussels in a frying pan on the barbecue, pour the wine over and lower the lid. Cook for 1–2 minutes, or until the mussels start to open.

Add the garlic and butter, and toss them through the mussels using tongs. Pour the cream and dill mixture over the mussels, then cover and cook for another minute, or until the mussels fully open. Toss to coat the mussels in the sauce, then discard any unopened mussels. Serve warm, sprinkled with the spring onion.

tomatoes stuffed with pistachio couscous

makes 8

200 g (7 oz) **instant couscous**

40 g (1½ oz) **butter**

100 g (3½ oz/⅔ cup) **currants**

1½ teaspoons grated **orange zest**

4 tablespoons **orange juice**

75 g (2½ oz/½ cup) **pistachio nuts**, roughly chopped

50 g (1¾ oz/½ cup) grated **parmesan cheese**

1 large handful **basil leaves**, chopped

8 firm **vine-ripened tomatoes**

Preheat a kettle or covered barbecue to low indirect heat.

Put the couscous in a heatproof bowl and pour on 500 ml (17 fl oz/2 cups) boiling water. Stir briefly, then cover and allow to stand for 5 minutes. Fluff up the grains with a fork, raking out any lumps, then stir the butter through. Add the currants, orange zest, orange juice, pistachios, parmesan and basil, then season with salt and freshly ground black pepper and mix well.

To prepare the tomatoes, cut about 1 cm (½ inch) off the tops to use as caps. Scoop out the seeds and pulp, and reserve for another use (see tip).

Carefully spoon the couscous stuffing into each tomato shell. Sit the tomatoes in a roasting tin, transfer to the barbecue, then lower the lid and cook for 15 minutes. Replace the tomato caps and cook for another 5 minutes, or until tender.

tip The tomato seeds and pulp can be chopped up and added to soups, risottos and tomato-based pasta sauces.

barbecued potato salad with salsa verde dressing

serves 4 as a side dish

1 kg (2 lb 4 oz) evenly sized **kipfler (fingerling) potatoes**,
scrubbed and peeled

3 tablespoons **olive oil**

2 **garlic cloves**, crushed

salsa verde dressing

1 tablespoon chopped **oregano leaves**

1 large handful **flat-leaf (Italian) parsley**

4 tablespoons **extra virgin olive oil**

3 **garlic cloves**, crushed

2 tablespoons **capers**, drained and rinsed

2 **anchovy fillets**, drained

1 tablespoon **lemon juice**

Preheat a kettle or covered barbecue to medium direct heat. Cut the potatoes in half on the diagonal. Toss them in a bowl with the oil and garlic and spread them on the barbecue grill. Lower the lid and cook the potatoes for 5 minutes on each side, or until cooked through — the exact cooking time will depend on the size of your potatoes.

While the potatoes are cooking, put the salsa verde dressing ingredients in a food processor and blend until smooth. Season to taste with salt and black pepper.

Put the potatoes in a serving bowl and toss the salsa verde through. Serve warm.

red vegetables with herb butter

serves 4 as a side dish

40 g (1¹/2 oz) **butter**, softened

3 tablespoons **basil leaves**, chopped

1 **red capsicum (pepper)**, quartered

2 small **beetroot**, quartered, or 4 **baby beets**, halved

4 **garlic cloves**, unpeeled

4 **cherry tomato trusses,** each with 3 tomatoes attached

2 tablespoons **oil**

4 **thyme sprigs**

4 tablespoons **vegetable stock**

In a small bowl, mix together the butter and basil and season with salt and freshly ground black pepper. Turn out onto a piece of foil and form into an 8 cm (3¹/4 inch) long log. Roll up tightly and freeze for 30 minutes.

Meanwhile, preheat a kettle or covered barbecue to low indirect heat.

Put the capsicum, beetroot, garlic cloves and the cherry tomato trusses in a large bowl. Drizzle with the oil, then lightly toss. Lay 4 large sheets of foil on a flat surface and divide the vegetable mixture evenly among the sheets. Add a sprig of thyme to each, then 1 tablespoon of stock and tightly fold up each parcel to secure.

Put the parcels on the barbecue grill, then lower the lid and cook for 30 minutes, or until the vegetables are tender. Cut the butter into 1 cm (¹/2 inch) thick slices, then open up the parcels and divide the butter among them while they're still on the barbecue. Cook for a further 1–2 minutes to melt the butter, then serve.

nugget pumpkins with goat's cheese and macadamia nuts

serves 4 as a side dish

2 x 350 g (12 oz) **nugget pumpkins**

1 tablespoon **oil**

40 g (1 1/2 oz) **baby rocket (arugula) leaves**

35 g (1 1/4 oz/1/4 cup) chopped **roasted macadamia nuts**

80 g (2 3/4 oz) **goat's cheese**, crumbled

honey mustard dressing

3 tablespoons **olive oil**

1 tablespoon **sherry vinegar**

2 teaspoons **wholegrain mustard**

1 teaspoon **honey**

Preheat a kettle or covered barbecue to medium indirect heat.

Wash the pumpkins thoroughly, then cut them in half horizontally and remove all the seeds. Rub the oil all over the flesh and place the pumpkins cut-side-up in a disposable foil tray. Season lightly with salt and freshly ground black pepper. Put the tray on the barbecue grill, then lower the lid and cook for 30 minutes, or until browned and soft — the cooking time will depend on the thickness of your pumpkins.

Meanwhile, put all the honey mustard dressing ingredients in a small screw-top jar. Shake well to combine and season to taste with salt and freshly ground black pepper.

Put the rocket, macadamia nuts and goat's cheese in a large bowl and gently mix together. Add the dressing and toss lightly to combine. Fill the cooked pumpkin halves with the salad mixture and serve immediately.

tip The skin of the pumpkins can be eaten in this recipe — just be sure to wash the pumpkins well before cooking.

tomato, olive and herb damper

serves 4 as a side dish

500 g (1 lb 2 oz/4 cups) **self-raising flour**

1 teaspoon **salt**

100 g (31/2 oz) **butter**, chopped

80 g (23/4 oz/1/2 cup) **semi-dried (sun-blushed) tomatoes**, chopped

100 g (31/2 oz/2/3 cup) **pitted kalamata olives**, roughly chopped

3 tablespoons snipped **chives**

3 tablespoons chopped **basil leaves**

170 ml (51/2 fl oz/2/3 cup) **milk**

plain (all-purpose) flour, for dusting

Preheat a kettle or covered barbecue to medium indirect heat.

Sift the flour and salt into a large bowl. Rub the butter into the flour with your fingertips until the mixture resembles fine breadcrumbs. Stir in the tomato, olives, chives and basil.

Make a well in the centre and add the milk and 125 ml (4 fl oz/1/2 cup) cold water. Using a cutting action, mix the liquid in with a knife until almost combined.

Turn the mixture out onto a lightly floured surface and lightly knead until a dough forms. Shape into a flat round loaf, dust the top with flour and, using a sharp knife, mark the top of the loaf into eight segments.

Sit the loaf on a floured tray and place in the middle of the barbecue. Lower the lid and cook for 50 minutes, or until the damper is well browned and cooked through. Serve warm with plenty of butter.

roasted potato cake

serves 6–8 as a side dish

oil, for brushing

250 g (9 oz/1 cup) **light sour cream**

3 tablespoons **milk**

1 kg (2 lb 4 oz) **all-purpose potatoes**

150 g (51/2 oz/11/4 cups) grated **cheddar cheese**

50 g (13/4 oz/1/2 cup) grated **parmesan cheese**

6 **spring onions (scallions)**, finely chopped

pinch of **cayenne pepper**

Preheat a kettle or covered barbecue to medium indirect heat. Brush a 26 cm (101/2 inch) round shallow cake tin with oil. Fold a 30 cm (12 inch) sheet of foil in half and use it to line the cake tin, running the edges up the sides of the tin. Brush the foil with oil, then line the base with a sheet of baking paper.

In a large bowl, stir the sour cream and milk together until smooth.

Peel the potatoes and slice them very thinly using a food processor or mandolin. Gently mix the potato through the sour cream mixture along with the cheddar, 4 tablespoons of the parmesan, the spring onion and cayenne pepper. Season well with salt and freshly ground black pepper.

Tip the mixture into the prepared tin, pressing down firmly with the back of a spoon. Scatter the remaining parmesan over the top and cover the tin with foil.

Put the tin on the barbecue, then lower the lid and cook the potato cake for 45 minutes. Remove the foil covering and continue baking for 45 minutes, or until the top of the potato is golden and crisp. Leave for 5 minutes, then gently loosen the cake out of the tin, using the foil wings as handles. Cut the potato cake into serving portions and serve hot.

desserts

a sweet ending

When people think of grilled foods, desserts don't generally spring to mind, but certain sweets turn quite delectable when treated to a blast of heat. And if the grill — be it heated from above or from underneath — is already hot from cooking savoury treats, it seems a shame not to put all that residual heat to good use. If you're using a barbecue hotplate for cooking a dessert, ensure it is completely spotless, otherwise your luscious-looking pancakes or crepes may be left with a suspicously garlicky or meaty aftertaste! So before you start cooking clean the grill well, scraping all the grit and burnt bits off, then wipe well with a damp cloth and rub with a cut lemon. This helps remove excess grease and flavours. Of course the alternative is to leave a small area of the hotplate clear to begin with, to save the hassle of cleaning it off. By this stage of cooking, the heat of the coal or fire barbecue will be much milder.

tasty tips

Most desserts only need a short cooking time, usually just to dissolve sugar or to melt ingredients such as butter or chocolate. Take care when grilling desserts as they generally have a high percentage of sugar, which means they will burn quickly if not checked frequently.

Fruit is a favourite contender for cooking on or under the grill as it holds its shape well. If you're threading it onto a skewer, opt for fruit that is slightly underripe so it won't fall apart during cooking. Securing the fruit on two skewers rather than a single skewer stops it slipping around during turning.

A wide assortment of fruits can be cooked on or under the grill. It is easier to grill harder fruits such as apples, pears or pineapples than fleshier fruits such as plums, peaches and nectarines, which become soft and mushy if cooked for too long or at too high a temperature. These fruits only need to be heated through, rather than cooked. They also hold their shape better if their skins are left on during grilling.

Sometimes the simplest desserts are the most superb. Take some melted butter, brush it over the best fruit of the season, sprinkle with your favourite spices such as cinnamon or nutmeg and a little soft brown sugar, then grill until deliciously golden brown and serve with yoghurt, ice cream, whipped cream or mascarpone cheese. So simple, so delicious.

grilled mango cheeks with coconut ice cream

serves 6

1 litre (35 fl oz/4 cups) **vanilla ice cream**, softened

30 g (1 oz/1/2 cup) **shredded coconut**, toasted

3 large ripe **mangoes**

2 tablespoons **soft brown sugar**

1 **lime**, halved

Mix the ice cream and coconut together in a large bowl, stirring only until just combined. Do not allow the ice cream to melt too much or it will become too icy. Return the mixture to the ice cream container and freeze for several hours, or overnight, until firm.

Preheat a barbecue flatplate, grill plate or chargrill pan to medium. Cut 2 cheeks off each mango, so you have 6 cheeks. If you prefer to serve the mangoes without their skins, scoop the cheeks away from the skin using a large spoon, then sprinkle the cheeks with the sugar. Alternatively, leave the skin on and score the flesh in a criss-cross pattern, then sprinkle the flesh with sugar.

Put the mango cheeks flesh-side-down on the barbecue and grill for 1–2 minutes, or until the sugar has caramelized. Divide the cheeks among six serving bowls and drizzle with a squeeze of lime. Add a scoop or two of coconut ice cream and serve.

tip The coconut ice cream is delicious served with any fruit combination. Try pineapple and bananas for a tropical flavour hit.

nectarine crumble with maple and lime syrup

serves 4

3 tablespoons **maple syrup**

1 teaspoon finely grated **lime zest**

4 ripe **nectarines**, cut in half, stones removed

30 g (1 oz/1/4 cup) **self-raising flour**

30 g (1 oz) **unsalted butter**, chilled and chopped

2 tablespoons **soft brown sugar**

Put the maple syrup and lime zest in a bowl. Stir well and leave to infuse for 15 minutes.

Heat the grill (broiler) to medium. Lightly brush the cut side of the nectarine halves with some of the syrup. Put the nectarine halves, cut-side-down, in a lightly oiled non-stick frying pan. Gently fry over low–medium heat for 1 minute on each side, or until slightly soft.

Put the flour in a small bowl and add the butter. Using your fingertips, rub the butter into the flour until the mixture resembles breadcrumbs, then stir through the sugar.

Sit the nectarines on the grill tray, cut-side-up. Lightly brush them with a little more syrup, then sprinkle the crumble mixture over the top and grill for 2 minutes, or until the crumble turns golden brown. Divide among four serving bowls and drizzle with the remaining syrup. Delicious served with vanilla ice cream.

waffles topped with soft meringue and lime and raspberry sauce

makes 4

lime and raspberry sauce
150 g (5 1/2 oz/1 punnet) **raspberries**
1 tablespoon **caster (superfine) sugar**
1 teaspoon finely grated **lime zest**

4 ready-made **waffles**
2 **egg whites**
80 g (2 3/4 oz/1/3 cup) **caster (superfine) sugar**

To make the lime and raspberry sauce, put the raspberries in a small saucepan with the sugar, lime zest and 2 tablespoons water. Simmer over low heat for about 3 minutes, stirring gently until the sugar has dissolved, taking care not to break up the raspberries. Set aside, but keep warm.

Heat the grill (broiler) to low. Put the waffles on the grill tray and grill for 30 seconds on each side, or until golden. Remove from the grill tray, but leave the grill on.

Beat the egg whites in a small bowl using an electric mixer until soft peaks form. Slowly add the sugar 1 tablespoon at a time, beating well after each addition, and scraping the sides of the bowl with a spatula between beatings. Continue beating until the meringue becomes thick and glossy — this will take about 3 minutes.

Using a large spoon or spatula, spread the meringue evenly all over each waffle, ensuring the entire surface is thickly covered. Gently swirl the meringue into little peaks, using the tip of your spoon or spatula.

Sit the waffles on the grill tray and grill for 3–5 minutes, or until the meringue peaks turn golden brown — watch them carefully to ensure they don't burn. Serve the waffles warm, drizzled with the lime and raspberry sauce.

Beat the egg whites until **smooth** and **glossy**, adding the sugar gradually.

Thickly **spread** the meringue over the waffles, **swirling** it into little peaks.

sweet drunken pineapple

serves 6

1 large **pineapple** or 2 small **pineapples**

oil, for brushing

40 g (1 1/2 oz/1/4 cup) coarsely grated **palm sugar** or **soft brown sugar**

2 1/2 tablespoons **rum**

2 tablespoons **lime juice**

3 tablespoons small **mint leaves**

thick (double/heavy) cream, to serve

Preheat a barbecue grill plate or chargrill pan (griddle) to medium. Trim the ends from the pineapple, remove the skin and cut into quarters lengthways. Brush the hot grill plate or chargrill pan with oil, add the pineapple quarters and cook for about 10 minutes, turning to brown the cut sides.

Take the pineapple off the heat and cut each quarter into 1.5 cm (5/8 inch) thick slices. Overlap the slices on a large serving plate.

Combine the sugar, rum and lime juice in a small jug, mixing well to dissolve the sugar. Pour the mixture evenly over the warm pineapple slices, then cover with plastic wrap and refrigerate for several hours. Serve at room temperature, sprinkled with the mint leaves and a dollop of cream.

flourless chocolate macadamia nut tart

serves 8

200 g (7 oz) good-quality **dark chocolate**, roughly chopped

200 g (7 oz) **unsalted butter**, chopped

165 g (5¾ oz/¾ cup) firmly packed **soft brown sugar**

4 **eggs**, lightly beaten

50 g (1¾ oz/⅓ cup) chopped **unsalted macadamia nuts**

thick (double/heavy) cream, to serve

fresh blueberries, to serve

Take the **chocolate**

off the heat to cool a little, then

whisk in the beaten eggs.

The mixture is **ready**

when it becomes smooth

and **glossy**.

Preheat a kettle or covered barbecue to medium–low indirect heat. Lightly brush the base and sides of a 24 cm (9$1/2$ inch) springform tin with oil and line the base with baking paper.

Put the chocolate, butter and sugar in a saucepan with 80 ml (2$1/2$ fl oz/$1/3$ cup) hot water. Stir over low heat until the chocolate and butter have both melted and the sugar has dissolved. Take off the heat and allow to cool slightly, then whisk in the eggs and chopped macadamia nuts. Stir until well combined and glossy.

Pour the mixture into the prepared tin and place in the middle of the barbecue. Lower the lid and cook for 1 hour 20 minutes, or until a skewer inserted into the middle of the tart comes out clean. Take the cake off the heat and leave to cool in the tin for 10 minutes. Release the sides of the tin, then cut the cake into slices. Serve warm or cold, with a dollop of cream and some fresh blueberries.

tip This tart is quite dense with a slightly wet texture when it is warm. When cool, it firms up and becomes fudge-like and easier to handle. The tart is equally delicious served cold or warm.

brioche with bananas and maple syrup

serves 4

4 **sugar** or **finger bananas**

2 tablespoons **soft brown sugar**

25 g (1 oz) **butter**, melted

1 tablespoon **orange juice**

2 **eggs**

125 ml (4 fl oz/1/2 cup) **milk**

185 ml (6 fl oz/3/4 cup) **maple syrup**

4 thick slices **brioche**

fresh blueberries, to serve

icing (confectioners') sugar, for dusting

Preheat a barbecue grill plate or flat plate to medium. Peel the bananas and cut them in half lengthways. Put the sugar, butter and orange juice in a small bowl and mix well until the sugar has dissolved. Brush the mixture evenly over the bananas on all sides.

In a bowl, whisk the eggs and milk together with 2 tablespoons of the maple syrup. Dip the brioche slices in the mixture, coating well on both sides.

Lightly brush the barbecue grill plate or flat plate with oil and cook the bananas and brioche for 2–3 minutes, or until the bananas are tender and both the brioche and bananas are nicely browned.

Divide the brioche among four serving bowls or plates. Sprinkle with blueberries, then arrange 2 banana halves on top. Drizzle with the remaining maple syrup, dust lightly with icing sugar and serve.

figs with amaretto mascarpone

serves 6

amaretto mascarpone

400 g (14 oz) **mascarpone cheese**

2 tablespoons **icing (confectioners') sugar**

2 tablespoons **amaretto liqueur**

25 g (1 oz/1/4 cup) **ground almonds**

1 tablespoon **demerara** or **soft brown sugar**

1/2 teaspoon **ground cinnamon**

9 **fresh figs**, halved

To make the amaretto mascarpone, put the mascarpone, icing sugar and amaretto in a bowl and mix together well. Cover and refrigerate for 15 minutes, or until cold.

Heat the grill (broiler) to high. In a small bowl, mix together the ground almonds, sugar and cinnamon. Sit the fig halves on the grill tray and sprinkle with the almond mixture. Grill for 3–4 minutes, or until the figs are hot, the sugar has melted and the tops are lightly browned. Serve hot, dolloped with the chilled mascarpone, allowing 3 fig halves per person.

crepes with ricotta and sour cherries

serves 4

crepe batter

90 g (3¼ oz/¾ cup) **plain (all-purpose) flour**

2 **eggs**

20 g (¾ oz) **butter**, melted

310 ml (11 fl oz/1¼ cups) **milk**

ricotta filling

375 g (13 oz/1½ cups) fresh **ricotta cheese**

80 g (2¾ oz/⅓ cup) **caster (superfine) sugar**

½ teaspoon finely grated **orange zest**

80 g (2¾ oz) **crème fraîche**

½ teaspoon **vanilla extract**

30 g (1 oz) **butter**, softened

80 g (2¾ oz/⅓ cup) **semi-dried (sun-blushed) sour cherries** (see tip)

topping

2 **eggs**

3 tablespoons **caster (superfine) sugar**

125 ml (4 fl oz/½ cup) **cream (whipping)**, lightly whipped

2 teaspoons **orange-flavoured liqueur**, such as Cointreau

icing (confectioners') sugar, for dusting

Gradually **whisk** the milk mixture into the flour to make a **lump-free** batter.

Put the filling along the bottom edge and **gently roll** up the crepe, tucking in the ends.

To make the crepe batter, sift the flour into a large bowl and make a well in the centre. In a separate bowl, mix together the eggs, butter and milk. Gradually whisk the milk mixture into the flour, beating well to make a smooth, lump-free batter. Strain to remove any lumps if necessary, then leave to stand for 10 minutes. Transfer to a jug for easier pouring.

While the batter is resting, make the ricotta filling. Put the ricotta, sugar, orange zest, crème fraîche, vanilla and butter in a bowl and mix until smooth. Stir in the cherries.

Heat the grill (broiler) to medium. Put a lightly greased 26 cm (10 1/2 inch) non-stick frying pan over medium heat. When the pan is hot, pour in a small amount of the crepe batter and swirl to thinly coat the base. Cook for 1–2 minutes, or until lightly browned, then flip the crepe over and brown the other side. Repeat with the remaining mixture to make 8 crepes.

Lay the crepes on a work surface. Divide the filling evenly among the crepes, placing it along the bottom edge in a narrow log and leaving a margin at each side of the filling. Gently roll up the crepes, tucking the sides in as you roll. Put the crepes in a large, shallow ovenproof dish or four individual ovenproof dishes and grill for 3–5 minutes, or until warmed through.

While the crepes are grilling, make the topping. Using an electric mixer, beat the eggs and sugar in a small bowl until light and fluffy. Fold in the cream and liqueur. Spoon the mixture over the warmed crepes, then return them to the grill and cook for about 5 minutes, or until golden brown. Dust with icing sugar and serve.

tip Semi-dried sour cherries are often available at speciality food stores.

caramelized pears

serves 4

4 ripe **corella pears**, or other **small sweet pears** (see tip)

4 tablespoons **demerara** or **soft brown sugar**

40 g (1½ oz) **butter**, softened

1 tablespoon **brandy**

200 g (7 oz) **crème fraîche**, to serve

4 **lemon wedges**, to serve

Heat the grill (broiler) to high. Peel the pears and halve them from top to bottom, keeping the stems intact if possible. Core the pears using a melon baller or a spoon.

Mix the sugar and butter together in a small bowl, then stir in the brandy. Sit the pears, cut-side-down, on the grill tray, and brush the tops with some of the sugar mixture. Grill for about 5 minutes, or until lightly browned.

Turn the pears, brush with a little more of the sugar mixture, then fill the cavities with the remaining mixture. Grill for another 3 minutes, or until the sugar is bubbling and brown. Baste again, then grill for a further 3 minutes.

Remove from the heat and leave the pears for 5 minutes, then serve with a scoop of crème fraîche, a squeeze of lemon juice and any juices from the grill tray.

tip If you are unable to obtain small pears, you could use 4 larger pears and increase the cooking time slightly.

nectarine and fig kebabs with rosewater syrup

serves 4

rosewater syrup

230 g (8 oz/1 cup) **caster (superfine) sugar**

2 teaspoons **rosewater**

1 tablespoon **lemon juice**

8 **nectarines**, cut in half, stones removed

8 **fresh figs**, cut in half

125 g (4½ oz/½ cup) **thick plain yoghurt**

2 tablespoons **honey**

2 tablespoons chopped **pistachio nuts**

To make the rosewater syrup, put the sugar in a saucepan with 250 ml (9 fl oz/1 cup) water. Stir, bring to the boil, then reduce the heat and simmer for 10 minutes. Remove from the heat and stir in the rosewater and lemon juice.

Soak eight bamboo skewers in cold water for 30 minutes. Thread a skewer through the side of a nectarine half, then a fig half, then another nectarine half and another fig half. Repeat to make 8 fruit kebabs. Put them in a large, flat non-metallic dish, then pour on the rosewater syrup. Cover and refrigerate for up to 3 hours.

Heat a barbecue flat plate to high and lightly brush with oil. When the plate is hot, cook the kebabs for 5 minutes, turning once, and brushing with a little more rosewater syrup during cooking. Put 2 kebabs on each serving plate, drizzle with the yoghurt and honey, sprinkle with the pistachios and serve.

french toast with vanilla yoghurt and fresh mango

serves 4

4 thick slices **two-day old brioche** or **panettone** (see tip)

3 **eggs**

60 ml (2 fl oz/1/4 cup) **milk**

10 g (1/4 oz) **unsalted butter**

1 **mango**, peeled and sliced

200 g (7 oz) good-quality **vanilla yoghurt**

1 teaspoon finely shredded **lime zest**

Preheat the barbecue flat plate to medium. Put the bread in a shallow dish large enough to hold all the slices at once without them overlapping. In a small bowl, whisk the eggs and milk until well combined, then pour the mixture over the bread and allow to soak for about 3 minutes.

Melt the butter on the hotplate. Add the bread slices and fry for 1–2 minutes on each side, or until golden brown. Transfer to four serving plates. Arrange the mango slices on top, add a dollop of yoghurt, sprinkle with lime zest and serve.

tip This is a great way to use up stale or leftover brioche or panettone. The bread should not be soft, otherwise it will become too mushy after grilling.

lime crème brûlée with raspberries

serves 4

500 ml (17 fl oz/2 cups) **cream (whipping)**

1 teaspoon finely grated **lime zest**

1/2 teaspoon **vanilla extract**

5 **egg yolks**

4 tablespoons **caster (superfine) sugar**

2 tablespoons **demerara** or **soft brown sugar**

150 g (51/2 oz/1 punnet) **raspberries**

Put the cream and lime zest in a saucepan and bring to the boil over low heat. Stir in the vanilla. Meanwhile, using an electric mixer, beat the egg yolks and caster sugar in a bowl until the sugar has dissolved and the mixture is light, thick and starts to hold its shape.

Beating slowly, gradually pour the hot cream into the egg mixture. Put in a double boiler or in a heatproof bowl over a pan of simmering water and stir for about 10 minutes, or until the mixture coats the back of a wooden spoon. Pour into four 125 ml (4 fl oz/1/2 cup) ramekins, then cover and refrigerate the custards overnight.

Heat the grill (broiler) to high. Sprinkle the demerara sugar evenly over the custards. Sit the ramekins in a shallow ovenproof dish, pack ice around them, then place the dish on the grill tray. Grill for 2 minutes, or until the sugar has melted, checking to see that it doesn't burn. Leave the ramekins in the ice for 1–2 minutes to allow the sugar to harden and the custards to set. Sit the raspberries on top and serve.

baumkuchen

serves 6

100 g (3 1/2 oz) **marzipan**

100 g (3 1/2 oz) **butter**, softened

80 g (2 3/4 oz/1/3 cup) **caster (superfine) sugar**, plus 2 tablespoons extra

1 teaspoon finely grated **lemon zest**

1 teaspoon **vanilla extract**

4 **eggs**, separated

60 g (2 1/4 oz/1/2 cup) **plain (all-purpose) flour**

60 g (2 1/4 oz/1/2 cup) **cornflour (cornstarch)**

2 tablespoons **apricot jam**, sieved and warmed

icing (confectioners') sugar, for dusting

fresh mixed berries, to serve

thick (double/heavy) cream (optional), to serve

glaze

100 ml (3 1/2 fl oz) **cream (whipping)**

140 g (5 oz) **dark chocolate**, chopped

Trim the edges of the cake, cut it into two rectangles and **spread** one half with jam.

Roll the remaining marzipan out **wafer thin** on a surface dusted with icing sugar.

Heat the grill (broiler) to high. Chop 30 g (1 oz) of the marzipan and put it in a small bowl with the butter and sugar. Beat with a hand-held electric mixer until light and fluffy, then beat in the lemon zest, vanilla and egg yolks. Sift in the flour and cornflour and stir until combined.

In a separate small bowl, beat the egg whites with an electric mixer until soft peaks form. Gradually add the extra 2 tablespoons of sugar, beating until dissolved. Fold the egg whites into the marzipan mixture in two batches.

Mark a 20 cm (8 inch) square on a sheet of baking paper, then spread 125 ml (4 fl oz/ 1/2 cup) of the cake mixture into the square. Put the sheet under the grill and cook for 1–2 minutes, or until the cake layer is well browned. Remove from the grill, allow to cool slightly, then spread the cake layer with another 125 ml (4 fl oz/1/2 cup) of the cake mixture. Return to the grill and cook again until well browned. Allow to cool slightly, then repeat the layering and grilling process until all of the mixture is used up. When you're finished, allow the cake to cool.

Trim the edges of the cake to form a neat square, then cut the cake in half to form two rectangles. Generously spread one of the rectangles with some of the jam, then sandwich the other half over the top. Trim if necessary to form a neat rectangle, then spread the rest of the jam over the top and sides.

Dust a work surface with icing sugar and thinly roll out the remaining marzipan until it is wafer thin. Use it to cover the top and sides of the cake, then sit the cake on a cake rack set in a tray.

To make the glaze, heat the cream in a small saucepan until almost boiling. Put the chocolate in a bowl, pour on the hot cream and stir gently until the chocolate has melted. Pour the chocolate mixture evenly over the top and sides of the cake, using a spatula to help spread the chocolate. Leave for about 30 minutes to set — it may be necessary to refrigerate the cake for a short time to set the chocolate.

Decorate the cake with fresh mixed berries, then cut into slices and serve cold, topped with a dollop of cream if desired.

sweet bruschetta

serves 4

250 g (9 oz/1 punnet) **strawberries**

200 g (7 oz) **ricotta cheese**

1 tablespoon **icing (confectioners') sugar**, plus extra to serve

2 teaspoons **Grand Marnier**, or other **orange-flavoured liqueur**

30 g (1 oz/1/4 cup) **toasted slivered almonds**

4 thick slices **panettone, pandoro** or **brioche**

2 tablespoons **soft brown sugar**

Heat the grill (broiler) to high. Reserve 4 small strawberries and chop the rest into 5 mm (1/4 inch) cubes. Put them in a bowl with the ricotta, icing sugar, Grand Marnier and almonds, and gently mix together.

Put the bread slices on the grill tray and grill for about 1 minute, or until golden brown on top. Turn the slices over, spread the ricotta mixture over the top and sprinkle with the sugar. Grill for about 45 seconds, or until the sugar has melted and the surface bubbles and browns. Transfer to a serving plate and dust lightly with icing sugar. Sit a reserved strawberry on each slice and serve hot.

blueberry custard crumbles

serves 6

300 g (10 1/2 oz/2 punnets) **blueberries**

1 **vanilla bean**

250 ml (9 fl oz/1 cup) ready-made **thick vanilla custard**

4 tablespoons **thick (double/heavy) cream**

2 tablespoons **icing (confectioners') sugar**, plus extra, for dusting

2 teaspoons finely grated **orange zest**

150 g (5 1/2 oz) **butternut biscuits (cookies)**

Divide the blueberries among six 185 ml (6 fl oz/3/4 cup) ramekins.

Split the vanilla bean in half lengthways, then scrape out the seeds and put them in a bowl (reserve the vanilla pod for another use). Add the custard, cream, icing sugar and orange zest and mix together well. Spoon the mixture over the berries.

Put the biscuits in a sealed bag and crush them with a rolling pin. Sprinkle the crumbs evenly over the custards and refrigerate for 1 hour.

Heat the grill (broiler) to medium. Dredge the tops of the crumbles generously with icing sugar and grill for about 2–3 minutes, or until lightly browned. Serve hot.

flavour
boosters

rubs

Rubs are dry or paste-like blends used to add flavour to meat without adding extra liquid. The quantities below will flavour 1 kg (2 lb 4 oz) of meat, enough to serve 4–6 people.

thai beef barbecue

Wash 6 coriander (cilantro) roots and their stems, then roughly chop and place in a food processor with 3 garlic cloves, 1 tablespoon freshly ground black pepper, 2 tablespoons vegetable oil, 1 tablespoon light soy sauce, 1 tablespoon dark soy sauce, 2 tablespoons fish sauce and 1 teaspoon sugar. Blend to a smooth paste. Smear the mixture over beef steaks and marinate in the refrigerator for several hours or overnight. Cook the steaks to your liking and serve them whole, or sliced and added to a Thai-style warm beef salad, sprinkled with 2 tablespoons finely chopped coriander (cilantro) leaves.

greek-style

Put 3 tablespoons lemon juice and 4 tablespoons olive oil in a small bowl with 1/2 teaspoon ground allspice, 2 tablespoons finely chopped oregano, 1 tablespoon finely chopped flat-leaf (Italian) parsley, 1 fresh torn bay leaf, 2 teaspoons finely chopped fresh ginger and 3 crushed garlic cloves. Season with freshly ground black pepper, rub all over your chosen meat and marinate for up to 1 hour. This rub is particularly delicious with lamb.

chermoula

Wash 40 g (1 1/2 oz/1/2 bunch) coriander (cilantro), including the roots and stems, and put in a food processor with 70 g (2 1/2 oz/1/2 bunch) flat-leaf (Italian) parsley, 3 garlic cloves, 2 teaspoons ground cumin, 1 teaspoon ground coriander, 2 teaspoons paprika, 1/4 teaspoon cayenne pepper, 4 tablespoons lemon juice and 125 ml (4 fl oz/ 1/2 cup) olive oil. Blend to a paste and rub the mixture over your chosen meat. Marinate for several hours, or overnight in the refrigerator.

hot and spicy chilli

In a bowl, mix together 2 tablespoons ground coriander, 1 tablespoon ground cumin, 2 teaspoons freshly ground black pepper, 2 tablespoons sweet paprika, 2 teaspoons chilli flakes and 2 teaspoons salt. Rub the mixture over your chosen meat and marinate for several hours or overnight. Best with red meats.

butters

Flavoured butters add a delicious taste and moistness to food without the hassle of making a sauce. These quantities are sufficient to coat 6–8 portions of meat or seafood.

fresh herb

In a small bowl, beat 125 g (4¹/2 oz) butter with a fork until soft. Stir in 1 tablespoon finely chopped flat-leaf (Italian) parsley, 2 teaspoons finely chopped thyme leaves and 2 teaspoons finely chopped oregano leaves and mix well. Scoop the mixture onto a sheet of plastic wrap and shape into a log about 13 cm (5 inches) long. Refrigerate for about 1 hour, or until firm. Slice into 1 cm (¹/2 inch) discs or spoon onto hot cooked meats or seafood.

Variations: To make **tarragon butter**, replace the thyme and oregano with 2 teaspoons finely chopped tarragon leaves and serve with cooked veal or chicken. To make a **dill butter**, replace the mixed herbs with 2 tablespoons finely chopped dill and serve with hot fish.

chilli and garlic

In a small bowl, beat 125 g (4¹/2 oz) butter with a fork until soft. Stir in 2 finely chopped and seeded small red chillies and 1 crushed garlic clove and mix well. Scoop the mixture onto a sheet of plastic wrap and shape into a log about 13 cm (5 inches) long. Refrigerate for about 1 hour, or until firm. Slice into 1 cm (¹/2 inch) discs or spoon onto hot cooked meats. This butter is especially suited to red meats.

chive and lemon

In a small bowl, beat 125 g (4¹/2 oz) butter with a fork until soft. Stir in 2 tablespoons chopped chives and 1 teaspoon finely grated lemon zest and mix well. Scoop the mixture onto a sheet of plastic wrap and shape into a log about 13 cm (5 inches) long. Refrigerate for about 1 hour, or until firm. Slice into 1 cm (¹/2 inch) discs or spoon onto hot fish or chicken.

seeded mustard

In a small bowl, beat 125 g (4¹/2 oz) butter with a fork until soft. Stir in 1 tablespoon seeded mustard and mix well. Scoop the mixture onto a sheet of plastic wrap and shape into a log about 13 cm (5 inches) long. Refrigerate for about 1 hour, or until firm. Slice into 1 cm (¹/2 inch) discs or spoon onto hot cooked red meats or salmon.

marinades

Marinating food makes it more tender and flavoursome. The quantities below will be enough for 1 kg (2 lb 4 oz) of your chosen meat and will serve 4–6 people.

teriyaki

Put 1 tablespoon sugar in a small saucepan with 125 ml (4 fl oz/1/2 cup) each of sake, mirin and dark soy sauce or shoyu. Bring to the boil, stir until the sugar has dissolved, then remove from the heat. Peel and finely grate a 2 cm (3/4 inch) piece of fresh ginger, and add it to the sauce with 2 crushed garlic cloves and 3 finely chopped spring onions (scallions). Mix well and allow to cool. Use the sauce to marinate your chosen meat for at least 20 minutes, or even overnight (drain the meat before cooking). If you wish, you can boil the drained marinade in a saucepan for 5 minutes to make a serving sauce.

tandoori

Peel and grate a 1 cm (1/2 inch) piece of fresh ginger. Put it in a small bowl with 2 tablespoons vegetable oil, 2 tablespoons paprika, 1 teaspoon ground cumin, 1 teaspoon ground turmeric, 1 teaspoon garam masala, 1/2 teaspoon ground ginger, 1/2 teaspoon ground cardamom,1/2 teaspoon cayenne pepper, 1/2 teaspoon ground coriander and 3 crushed garlic cloves. Stir in 125 g (41/2 oz/1/2 cup) thick plain yoghurt and 2 teaspoons lemon juice and mix well. Use the mixture to marinate meat or seafood in the refrigerator for at least 4 hours, or preferably overnight. This marinade is particularly good with lamb and poultry.

thai coconut

In a small non-metallic bowl, combine 400 ml (14 fl oz) coconut cream, 2 teaspoons grated fresh ginger, 1 crushed garlic clove, 2 tablespoons lime juice, 2 finely chopped and seeded red chillies, 2 tablespoons chopped coriander (cilantro) leaves and 1 finely chopped lemon grass stem (white part only). This marinade works well with white meat, fish or seafood.

lime and ginger

Put 125 ml (4 fl oz/1/2 cup) lime juice in a small non-metallic bowl with 1 tablespoon grated fresh ginger, 1 crushed garlic clove and 2 tablespoons oil and mix well. This is a lovely marinade for chicken, fish or seafood.

bastes

Brush bastes over meat or seafood sparingly at the start of cooking and apply more heavily after the meat has cooked through. If the meat has been marinated in the baste, do not apply any more baste after the meat has been taken off the heat as the raw meat juices can contain dangerous bacteria. The quantities below will baste 6–8 portions of fish or meat.

south-western barbecue

In a saucepan, mix together 4 tablespoons tomato passata (puréed tomatoes), 3 tablespoons tomato ketchup, 2 tablespoons chilli sauce, 1 tablespoon soft brown sugar, 1 tablespoon cider vinegar, 3 crushed garlic cloves, 1 teaspoon garlic salt and 1/2 teaspoon hickory salt or smoky paprika. Stir over low heat until the sugar has dissolved, then simmer for 8–10 minutes, stirring occasionally. Allow the mixture to cool, then stir in 2 tablespoons oil. Brush over your chosen meat before and during cooking. This baste is suited to pork ribs and can be made up to 1 week ahead of time.

balsamic

Put 125 ml (4 fl oz/1/2 cup) balsamic vinegar in a small non-metallic bowl with 2 tablespoons olive oil, 3 tablespoons lemon juice, 2 tablespoons soft brown sugar, 1 crushed garlic clove and a generous grind of black pepper. Stir until the sugar has dissolved and brush over your chosen meat before and during cooking. This baste is particularly lovely with chicken.

sweet chilli

In a small non-metallic bowl, mix together 125 ml (4 fl oz/1/2 cup) Thai sweet chilli sauce, 2 tablespoons lime juice, 1 tablespoon fish sauce and 1 tablespoon soft brown sugar. Mix well to dissolve the sugar and brush over your chosen meat before and during cooking. This baste is delicious with chicken, pork, seafood and firm tofu.

honey and mustard

Put 3 tablespoons honey in a small non-metallic bowl with 2 tablespoons Dijon mustard, 1 tablespoon wholegrain mustard, 1 tablespoon oil and 1 tablespoon lemon juice. Mix well and brush over your chosen meat before and during cooking. This baste is suitable for most meats.

crusts

These are not your traditional crusts, but a crisp coating that forms on the surface of the meat or fish during cooking. For best results, cook the meat or fish on a lightly oiled grill plate or flat plate. The quantities given here will coat 6–8 portions of meat or fish.

classic peppercorn

Coarsely crush 6–8 tablespoons black peppercorns in a mortar with a pestle. Season with sea salt and pat onto steak or other red meat. To vary the recipe, you could also use a mixture of white and pink peppercorns.

coriander and cumin

Coarsely crush 4 tablespoons coriander seeds and 2 tablespoons cumin seeds in a mortar with a pestle. Season with sea salt flakes and freshly ground black pepper, then press onto lightly oiled meat such as red meats and salmon cutlets.

chilli, lime and lemon grass

Put 2 finely chopped large red chillies in a food processor with 3 chopped lemon grass stems (white part only), 1 tablespoon finely grated lime zest, 4 finely chopped makrut (kaffir lime) leaves, 4 tablespoons soft brown sugar, 4 tablespoons oil and a large handful of coriander (cilantro) leaves. Blend to a fine paste. Spread over meat, chicken or fish and cook over medium heat to prevent burning.

dukkah

Put 2 tablespoons coriander seeds and 1 tablespoon cumin seeds in a small frying pan. Dry-fry over medium heat for 1–2 minutes, or until fragrant. Allow to cool, then place in a mortar or spice mill with 2 teaspoons dried thyme. Pound or grind into a coarse mixture, then transfer to a small bowl. Put 100 g (3½ oz/⅔ cup) sesame seeds in a small frying pan and dry-fry over medium heat for 2–3 minutes, or until lightly browned. Allow to cool, then add to the spice mixture with 100 g (3½ oz/ 1 cup) ground almonds. Mix well, then press onto lightly oiled meat.

index

pork and polenta stack 255
vietnamese pork kebabs with
    chilli lime pickle 219
warm chinese pork with radish
    salad 96
potatoes
    bacon and potato skewers with
        tarragon cream 148
    barbecued potato salad with salsa
        verde dressing 330
    potato rösti with bacon and sage
        268
    roasted potato cake 338
    roasted rosemary potatoes with
        red capsicum aïoli 152
    smoked trout and kipfler potato
        salad 290
prawns
    caesar salad with grilled king
        prawns 215
    honey and lime prawn kebabs with
        mango salsa 24
    marinated prawns with mango
        chilli salsa 236
pumpkin with saffron and coriander
    butter 263
pumpkins with goat's cheese and
    macadamia nuts, nugget 334

quail
    quail with a herb butter stuffing
        and rocket salad 115
    spiced quail with grilled plums 84

rainbow trout with salmon roe
    butter 220
ratatouille, creamy, with farfalle 72
red vegetables with herb butter 333
roasted potato cake 338
roasted rosemary potatoes with red
    capsicum aïoli 152

rolled fish fillets with lemon dill
    cream 309
rosemary and pepper rib-eye steaks
    with olive oil mash 239
rosemary-smoked lamb rack with
    minted broad beans 321
rubs 384

sage and bocconcini pots 35
salad pizzas 67
salads
    caesar salad with grilled king
        prawns 215
    carrot and almond salad 127
    eggplant, tahini and mint salad 260
    fresh ricotta with capsicum and
        chilli salad 259
    grilled pancetta, haloumi and
        cherry tomato salad 136
    mushroom and spinach salad with
        quick pesto dressing 144
    niçoise salad with fresh tuna 227
    side salad of grilled mixed
        vegetables 147
    summer salad with marinated tofu
        steaks 203
    warm mediterranean lamb salad 194
salmon, ricotta and red onion frittata 43
satay, lamb 107
sausages
    chevapcici 123
    chipolatas with sage and pancetta
        and fresh tomato salsa 235
    chorizo and haloumi skewers 184
    gourmet sausage sandwiches 216
    sausage skewers with lemon olive
        salsa 64
    sausage and sweet potato wraps 44
    split sausages with caramelized
        onions and a gorgonzola
        topping 100

First published by 2005 by Murdoch Books Pty Limited
This edition published in 2010

Murdoch Books Australia
Pier 8/9, 23 Hickson Road, Millers Point NSW 2000
Phone: +61 (0)2 8220 2000 Fax: +61 (0)2 8220 2558
www.murdochbooks.com.au

Murdoch Books UK Limited
Erico House, 6th Floor North, 93–99 Upper Richmond Road
Putney, London SW15 2TG
Phone: + 44 (0) 20 8785 5995 Fax: + 44 (0) 20 8785 5985
www.murdochbooks.co.uk

Chief Executive: Juliet Rogers
Publishing Director: Kay Scarlett

Publisher: Lynn Lewis
Senior Designer: Heather Menzies
Project Managers: Paul McNally, Rachel Carter
Photographer: Jared Fowler, Stuart Scott (cover)
Stylist: Cherise Koch, Louise Bickle (cover)
Designer: Tracy Loughlin
Production: Kita George

National Library of Australia Cataloguing-in-Publication Data
Title: Grill it.
ISBN 9781741966435 (pbk.).
Series: It series (Sydney, NSW) Notes: Includes index.
Subjects: Barbecue cookery. Grill pans.
Dewey Number: 641.76

PRINTED IN CHINA

IMPORTANT: Those who might be at risk from the effects of salmonella poisoning (the elderly, pregnant women, young children and those suffering from immune deficiency diseases) should consult their doctor with any concerns about eating raw eggs.